D1603495

March 1996

To Chris—

We all thank you for being
what we all have been taught what
the Real West is and always has
been. You represent a part of
our heritage that has been lost
in this country, & I must commend
you for living the life you love
and being the person you wish
to be. You are, Chris, a rare
breed. I admire your tremendous
abilities & your drive to accomplish
the best in your field. I am
proud to be considered one of
your friend — Steve Frie

Cowboy Culture

The Last Frontier of American Antiques

Michael Friedman

Schiffer Publishing Ltd

1469 Morstein Road, West Chester, Pennsylvania 19380

Title page photo:
The "Teddy Roosevelt" bridle, made for and presented to President Theodore Roosevelt to commemorate his famous American regiment in the Spanish-American war of 1898. It has American flags and the words ROUGH RIDERS spelled out in the noseband, and glass rosettes with a "T" and an "R" at the corners of the browband. Collection: High Noon.

Cover background:
Detail of fine leatherwork on a saddle by E.H. Bohlin, circa 1930s. Collection: Thomas W. Connally

Cover photo:
Hamley spotted angora batwing chaps with card suits. Collection: Michael Friedman.

Back cover:
Early half seat saddle with Sam Stagg rigging. This saddle has just about everything a "cowboy" collector could ask for. It is signed "D.B. Curtis, Deadwood, D.T." (Dakota Territory). Signed territorial saddles are rare, but ones with names like "Deadwood" add a dimension of having come from one of the most colorful and well known towns of the Old West. Curtis was listed in the Deadwood directory as a saddle maker in the years 1876-1877, and supposedly came from Cheyenne where he was believed to have worked for Gallatin. Photo: Steve Brown. Collection: Michael Friedman.

Published by Schiffer Publishing, Ltd.
1469 Morstein Road
West Chester, Pennsylvania 19380
Please write for a free catalog.
This book may be purchased from the publisher.
Please include $2.00 postage.
Try your bookstore first.

Copyright © 1992 by Michael Friedman.
Library of Congress Catalog Number: 91-67012.

All rights reserved. No part of this work may be reproduced or used in any forms or by any means— graphic, electronic or mechanical, including photo- copying or information storage and retrieval systems— without written permission from the copyright holder.

Printed in the United States of America.
ISBN: 0-88740-379-4

We are interested in hearing from authors with book ideas on related topics.

P.S.

You are what he would call like to be. A part of the myth & the legend of the cowboy

FOR JENNY AND ZOE

and the American West. It's hard work & you do it damn well. I pray that you will be able to keep the lifes you have and fulfill the part of your life that is missing. Best of luck —

Your friend
Stewart

Child's deer hide batwing chaps with colorful inlaid leather belt
and wings. Circa 1930s. Collection: Michael Friedman.

Acknowledgments

I would like to thank the members of the National Bit, Spur, and Saddle Collectors Association for their support and encouragement in this project. I only wish I could have included examples from all the members who expressed an interest in having their items included. Time, travel and budget precluded many wonderful and deserving items from being pictured. I would also like to thank the members of the Texas Gun Collectors Association.

I have learned that cowboy and Western collectors as a group are not investors or speculators. Their love of the material and the romance and history of the Old West is what drives them to their next acquisition.

Thanks go to Enrique Guerra, Claude Lyle, Vic and Betty Williams, Joe Gish, Jim Holley, Roger Baker, Jim and Theresa Brown, George Pitman, Joseph Sherwood and Linda Kohn for sharing their incredible collections, their hospitality and willingness to let me photograph their treasures.

Thanks to Lang Spraggins, Joe Goodson, Ernie Hoodenpyle, Tom Connally, Bruce Thalberg, Michael Garlenski, Jerry Jordan, Ken Schatra, Dominick Cervone, Tom Burks, Mark Hooper, Joel and Kate Kopp, Bill Adamson, Dick Engle, William Williamson, Ron Van Anda, Roger Lebert, Bob Hunn, Ed Vebell, James MacKie, Alex Shear, J. Boessenecker, Gene and Cathy Gavin, Marvin Pruitt, Jim and Carole Statler, Dave VanMeter, Steve Hofheimer, Ruth and Jerry Murphy, Jack Ringwalt, Allan Katz, Dave Wooley, Dennis Kurlander, John Kubicki, Kathy and Stuart Levinson, James Kronen, Ken Bartlett, Bob Adams, Brad Witherell, Brian Lebel, and Paul Stuckey.

Special thanks to Doug Deihl and Tom and Ginny Dawes.

All photos by Michael Friedman, except where noted.

Front cover photograph: Tom Dawes
Back cover photograph: Steve Brown
High Noon Horsehair collection: Victoria Mihich

Trailtown, Cody, Wyoming.

Preface

Surprisingly little has been published about the Old West category of Americana. While the early period lasted a relatively short time (from 1840 to 1910), there exists a large body of extraordinary items relating to the Old West. So large, in fact, that this volume can only hope to survey what has been collected. My intention is to offer a broad view of objects which reflect the range of Western antiques in terms of both type and quality. I have, for the most part, limited myself to private collections, so that most of what is included has not been previously published. These collections are intensely personal and reflect the special interests of each collector. It is not surprising that much of what is shown comes from Texas collections, since Texas is to the Old West collector what New England is to the early-American collector.

One remarkable aspect of the Old West is that there are still living people who are only one generation from the major events of the period—people whose grandfathers rode with Jesse James, or were in Tombstone in 1881 when the gunfight at the O.K. Corral took place. The advent of automobiles and airplanes has made these events seem so long ago, but in fact outlaws on horses were holding up trains in this century. There are still numerous ghost towns which dot the western landscape; entire towns abandoned as the country grew and moved away from cattle trails and mining centers of the late 19th century. While life in the Old West has been wildly idealized and romanticized, the fact remains that towns like Dodge City,

Rusty relic of a colt single action Army revolver. Found loaded in a locked position with 7 notches on barrel, this gun appears to have gone down in a shootout. Collection: C.W. Lyle, Jr.

Tombstone, and Deadwood actually did exist, complete with outlaws and marshals, with gamblers and soiled doves and cowboys who, for about $30 a month, drove the cattle north from Texas to the Kansas railheads. Unattended herds of cattle roamed throughout Texas during the war, and at it's conclusion many of those returning found work in rounding up and transporting cattle to the railheads in Kansas. 1000 miles, at 12 miles a day, took 3 months of walking from Texas to Kansas. While the trail drives lasted only 15 years, this period proved to be the golden age of the cowboy. The height of the Texas trail drives took place in 1871 when an estimated 700,000 cattle were driven to the Kansas plains.

The average cowboy often had to make his own embellishments and decorations and here we find folk art of the common man. His imagination and uniqueness made each modest possession an expression of personal style. Because cowboys were essentially itinerant and poor, they had few possessions, and because these items were utilitarian, every man's gear was extremely important to him. Since most cowboys owned only what would fit in their saddlebags, relatively little from this period has survived. Photographs show cowboys sitting around a campfire with a pile of spurs, each inspecting the special differences and decoration. As one might expect, each geographic area created its own unique styles.

When we see the Hollywood version of western life, we seldom get a sense of the hardships endured. The Montana snows (before down parkas), the ever-present diseases (before penicillin), the 120 degrees of heat in the west Texas desert, and the constant threat of outlaws and hostile Indians. Imagine a life filled with both the majesty of the Rocky Mountains and endless grassy plains as a setting for the daily courage required to meet unknown dangers. Imagine wagon trains forging trails west to California in 1849 to take part in the greatest of all American dreams, the Gold Rush. For every "winner" there were 1000 "losers," but they shared the dream that we share today and the freedom to pursue that dream, and that is what America is all about.

This book is dedicated to the dreamers, to the cowboys. If it succeeds, it will be by acting as a mirror which reflects the images of cowboy dreams, the irrepressible creative expression of those dreamers. It will open a window to the part of our history that personifies the American spirit of ingenuity and artistic spontaneity.

As with all art, fine or applied, the pictures tell the story, the words can only explain and clarify.

This period so fascinates people that even today one can travel the west and find modern day cowboys who work long hours for subsistence wages but would never give up the cowboy life for any other. I know wranglers in Wyoming and Texas who are as committed to their cowboy life as the men who preceded them by a hundred years. They love being cowboys, they love the land and they know that they are the last of a vanishing breed. The golden age of the cowboy was truly the last period of Americana, before the machine age forever changed the way we lived. Those of us who never outgrew our childhood dreams of the Old West will protect its treasures for posterity.

Contents

Introduction

Texas was Mexico before it was Texas. Spanish settlers brought horses and cattle to Mexico some 400 years ago. In Spain, cattle were not allowed to roam free because space was limited. However, in the vastness of the New World, they were set free to graze and reproduce. Soon there were huge herds and large Spanish ranches throughout northern Mexico. The Spanish trained local Indians to ride horses and work the cattle. They became known as *vaqueros,* from the Spanish word *vaca,* which means cow. This is where the legend begins.

In a very real sense, the first cowboy was a *vaquero.* When the Spanish brought cattle north to what is now Texas, they were dressed in chaps, [*chaperaras,* pronounced shaps] spurs, and broad brimmed hats [*sombreros*] to protect them from the sun. Their outfits had evolved over a long period of spanish history, and were both ornate and objects of pride and stature. Their spurs were large and elaborate and their saddles embroidered and mounted in silver. The higher on the economic scale, the more ornate and distinctive were their garments. This was true of the American cowboy as well; ranchers and successful businessmen had saddles that were finely carved and tooled, boots with silver engraved heels and toes, and guns with beautifully engraved designs and pearl or ivory grips. The lower on the economic ladder, the more basic were the decorations.

Very unusual Bowie knife with a silver mounted ivory handle of a coiled snake. There is no makers mark, but it is believed to have been custom made in Louisiana around 1850. Collection: Enrique Guerra.

I have been told that 600,000 cattle came up to eastern Kansas and southeastern Nebraska in 71', Lincoln Nebraska being the north end of the trail, because there were no ranches above that point; only Indians and buffalo.

We Pointed Them North

Opposite page:
An open rigging saddle, circa 1883, made by Ellis and Kelner of 411 S. Jennings, Fort Worth, TX and stamped in 13 places. The cast iron stirrups with inlaid bronze are marked "Fort Worth." Marked Texas saddles from this period are rare and this one is about as good as they get. Collection: C.W. Lyle, Jr.

Chapter One

Spurs

Spurs originally were brought to the New World by Spanish settlers in the 16th century. The modern period of spurs lasted from about 1860 to 1910. During this period the Mexican spur contained many interesting design elements mixing silver and iron to create figural, as well as geometric, works of art. They were typically large and heavy and were sometimes adorned with semi-precious stones such as rubies and emeralds.

Another style spur evolved from the Mexican tradition in Texas. It's characteristics can be traced north along the length of the cattle trails to Kansas, Oklahoma, Colorado, Wyoming, Missouri and Montana. Texas style spurs didn't have jingle bobs, and the finer examples were decorated with silver overlay often exhibiting steerheads, suits of cards, or a lady's leg. The examples shown here serve not only to document the cowboy's life, but also show important differences between the artistic visions of the makers and the social positions of the owners.

Opposite page:
Colt's "Arm of the law" or "Tex—Patches", as it is affectionately known by collectors, is one of the more popular firearms advertisements, even though it is not considered rare. The original painting was done by Frank E. Schoonover in 1925. Collection: Roger Baker.

Pair of double mounted inlaid Cañon City Prison spurs, with spur straps, marked "Issac Cherry, Durango, Colorado." The spurs were made in the 1920s or 1930s in the Canyon City Prison, Canyon City, Colorado; the spur straps were probably made around 1900. Canyon City spurs often include the prisoner's number stamped on the heel band. Collection: Jim Holley.

Nicely executed example of Cañon City Prison spurs. Typical of prison-made spurs are the inlaid rowels, circa 1900 to 1930. Collection: Dick Engle.

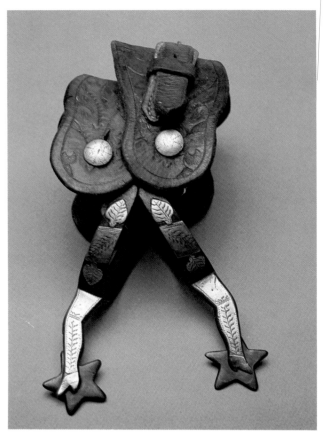

Gal-leg spurs with star-shaped rowels, made by C.P. Shipley of Kansas City, Missouri. Collection: C.W. Lyle, Jr.

Gold and silver double gal-leg spurs. Heart shaped buttons and cookie-cutter rowels add to the beauty of these McChesneys, circa 1920s. The large gold and silver bronco rider concho is by Visalia of San Francisco. Collection: C.W. Lyle, Jr.

McChesney gal-leg spur in new condition with the original box. McChesney was born in 1867 in South Bend, Indiana. After moving to Paul's Valley, Oklahoma, in 1907 he opened what was to become the largest bit and spur factory in the world. He died in 1928. The McChesney Company was bought by The Nacona Boot Co. of Nacona, Texas. Model T axles were utilized in the production of some of these spurs. Collection: C.W. Lyle, Jr.

Beautifully proportioned silver overlay spurs by Snitker of Gillett, Wyoming, circa 1910 to 1930, with spectacular rowels. Snitker's work was illustrated and sold in Bohlin catalogs. Collection: Dick Engle.

Fine pair of peacock motif spurs set with rubies and emeralds, circa 1920s, made by J.R. McChesney. Collection: C.W. Lyle, Jr.

Like the Colt Peacemaker, spurs are an icon of the Old West. The very sight of an old cowboy spur automatically conjures images that transcend the form. The infinite variations, the artistry of the maker's hand, the statement that was made by the wearer, all combine to make this an exciting subject. The spurs pictured on the following pages are some of the most beautiful ever made. From the Mexican *vaquero* to the Wyoming wrangler, the evolution of a cowboy's spurs can best be related visually.

Interesting pair of silver mounted Kelly Bros. spurs with open iron work, engraved conchos and early leathers, circa 1920s Collection: C.W. Lyle, Jr.

The only thing to do during a stampede was to ride in the lead of the cattle-not in front, but alongside-and try to head them and get them into a mill, because once they got to milling they would stop running after a while. And that was the reason for singing or making some kind of noise when we were riding with a stampede, because if you could hear your partner you knew he was all right, but if you couldn't hear him he might be down. And if that happened, you stopped trying to mill them, and let them run in a straight direction to get away from him.

We Pointed Them North

Wonderful, detailed decorative work distinguish these spurs made by August Buermann. They are marked with a star and "AB" on the inside. Collection: Dick Engle.

The inlaid large rowels on this pair of prison-made spurs add to their already strong visual impact, circa 1920s. Collection: C.W. Lyle, Jr.

Mark of spurs at right.

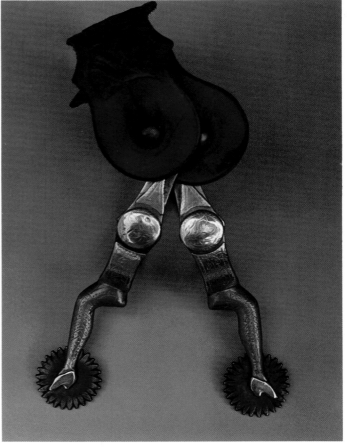

Finely formed pair of gal-leg spurs by G.A. Bischoff & Co. of Gainesville, Texas, circa 1910, with gold, silver and copper overlay. Collection: James Statler.

Pair of Texas spurs with silver heart buttons and silver chevrons on shanks and heel bands. Circa 1930. Collection: C.W. Lyle, Jr.

Unusual and beautiful pair of Texas spurs with silver overlay bearing the owner's initials and extra large and fancy 10 point rowels, circa 1900 to 1920, made by J. O. Bass, Tulia, Texas. Collection: Dick Engle.

Typical Texas style spurs, this pair was made by Adolf Bayers, circa 1940s to 1950s. Bayers made a lot of spurs for West Texas cowboys, many of them with silver overlay decoration indicating either the ranch brand or cowboy's initials. Collection: C.W. Lyle, Jr.

No. 189 "The Pendleton" spurs with 20 point rowels, marked "Crockett" on the inside, from Kansas City, Missouri, circa 1920s. The band has an interesting rawhide "shim" added by a former owner. Strap conchos are affixed by 24 individually added spots on each concho. Collection: Bill Adamson.

The Colorado State Penintentiary at Cañon City had a very effective crafts program devoted to spurs, bits, and other types of cowboy gear. This unmarked pair of spurs with inlaid nickel silver in both the heel band and rowels is a classic example of this work. Collection: Roger Baker.

Early Bianchi style "bottle opener" spurs with 8-point rowels, double mounted, Mexican coins on buttons and rowel pins. "Crocket" marked on inside. Made circa 1900-1910 if by Arthur Crockett and circa 1910-1915 if by Oscar Crockett. Collection: Bill Adamoon.

A pair of J.O. Bass spurs, circa 1920, with card suits mounted on one side. The old spur straps have brass buckles. There is the number "290" in the heel band, along with the maker's name J.O. Bass of Tulia, Texas. The name "H. Hickman" is stamped on the inside of the shank, probably denoting the person for whom the spurs were made. Bass was born in Georgia in 1880, and moved to Tulia, Texas in 1905. Tom Mix wore his spurs, as did many Texas Rangers. He worked until 1924. Collection: Jim Holley.

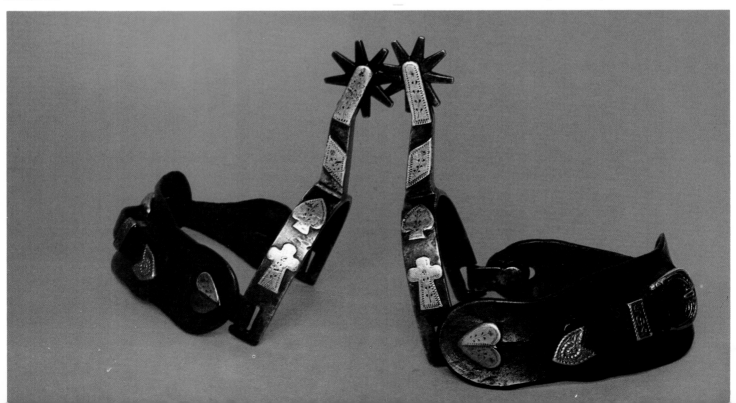

"Four Hearts" spurs with 16 point rowels. " O. Crockett" is marked inside the band, probably from Kansas City, Missouri, possibly Pawhuska, Oklahoma, circa 1915, but certainly in the period of 1910-1920. They were made by Oscar Crockett for Leo Carillo, who had a career in Wild West Shows, motion pictures and television. Collection: Bill Adamson.

"Four Hearts" spurs with 12 point rowels, made by Bill Adamson of Kersey, Colorado, circa 1991. One of some half dozen pairs of "Four Hearts" spurs in varying sizes that have been made by Adamson intentionally smaller than O. Crockett's "Pancho" spurs, but bigger than a typical "Four Hearts" spur. Adamson is among the few contemporary spurmakers whose work is collected. Collection: Bill Adamson.

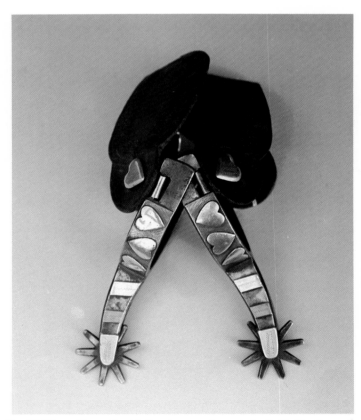

No. 1070 "Four Hearts" spur with 10 point rowels made by August Buermann Manufacturing Company of Newark, New Jersey. Marked "Hand Forged Steel", "Patent" star, outside band under the button, circa 1900 to 1925, possibly earlier. These are very well made, a little smaller than the typical "Four Hearts," but still a man's spur. Collection: Bill Adamson.

No. 70 "Four Hearts" with 9 point rowel, made by Kelly Brothers of Dalhart, Texas or El Paso, Texas, circa 1920s. Collection: Bill Adamson.

Beautiful pair of gal-leg, Bull-head spurs with ruby eyes and 13 point rowels, made by J.R. McChesney, circa 1920s. These are very hard to find and desirable. Collection C.W. Lyle, Jr.

Double gal-leg gold and silver spurs, circa 1920s, made by J.R. McChesney. Note the silver and gold horsehead concho and suit of cards on the button. Collection: C.W. Lyle, Jr.

Bottle-opener, shank-style spurs, circa early 1900s, made by C. P. Shipley of Kansas City, Missouri, and stamped with his mark on the inside of the heel band. Charles Shipley was born in Wooster, Ohio in 1864 and later founded his own company in Kansas City in 1885. He died in 1943. Collection: Vic Williams.

Very fine and scarce pair of Qualey Bros. spurs. The Qualeys worked in Joseph, Idaho and these spurs date to 1932 when they were made for Ray Holes who worked for Qualey for 30 years as a saddle tree maker. Collection: James Statler.

Special order spurs of 10K gold and silver mountings with gold and nickel rowels and 9 point rowels. Marked "Crockett" on inside, made in Kansas City, Missouri, circa 1930-1935. In mint condition, these are said to once have been traded for a shetland pony. Collection: Bill Adamson.

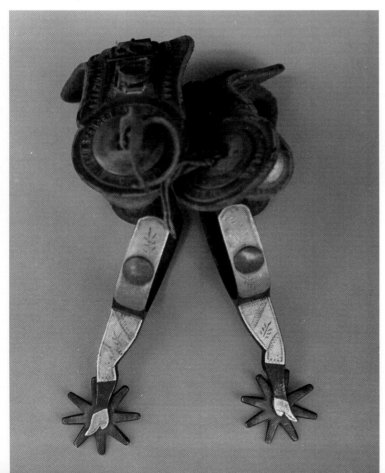

Double mounted gal-legs spurs with heavy patina and 8 point rowels. The early leathers are marked "Hibbard Spencer Bartlett and Company, Chicago, Illinois." They were made by Oscar Crockett, probably in Kansas City, Missouri, circa 1915-1916. Crockett was born in Pecos, Texas in 1887. He went on to become one of the most successful spurmakers of all time. He died in 1949. Collection: Bill Adamson.

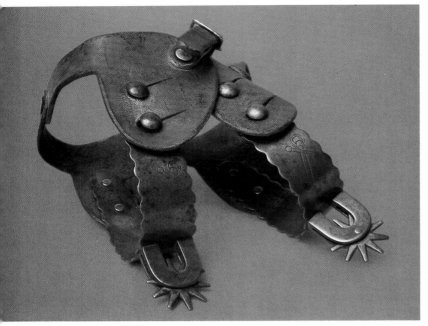

Eureka scalloped spurs, circa 1870, believed to have been made by the North and Judd Mfg. Co. Note the large stamped anchor and original harness style straps. Collection: Vic Williams.

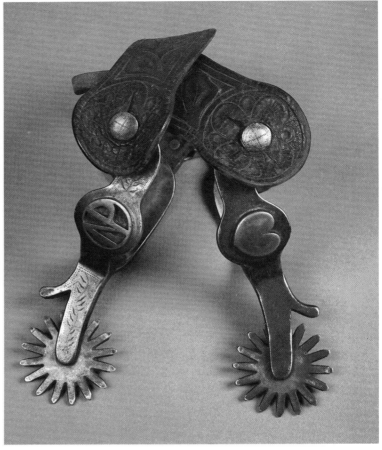

Texas-style spurs made by Crockett with brass heart applied to one side and the cowboy's initials to the other. Collection: Michael Friedman.

Crude forged spurs mounted with stamped copper on one side and silver with turquoise settings on the other. The swinging buttons have stamped silver and copper overlays, and the rowels were hand filed, circa 1940. Probably made by a Navajo Indian, the turquoise stones on this pair are very unusual and, though crude in execution, give these spurs a unique charm. Ex-collection H. C. Lewis. Collection: Douglas Deihl.

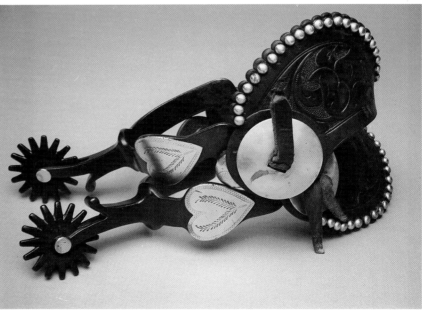

Nice pair of Kelly Bros. heart motif spurs, signed on the outside and rear of the band with 16 point rowels. Kelley Bros. are one of the best known spurmakers of all and worked in different combination of partnerships from 1911 to 1965. Collection: C.W. Lyle, Jr.

An interesting pair of gold eagle-head spurs with silver overlay suits of cards on the bands and engraved iron work on the shanks, circa 1915-1920, made by J.R. McChesney, Pauls Valley, Oklahoma. Collection: C.W. Lyle, Jr.

Bischoff gal-leg spurs with rare locking rowel feature. Bischoff worked in Gainesville Texas. Collection: C.W. Lyle, Jr.

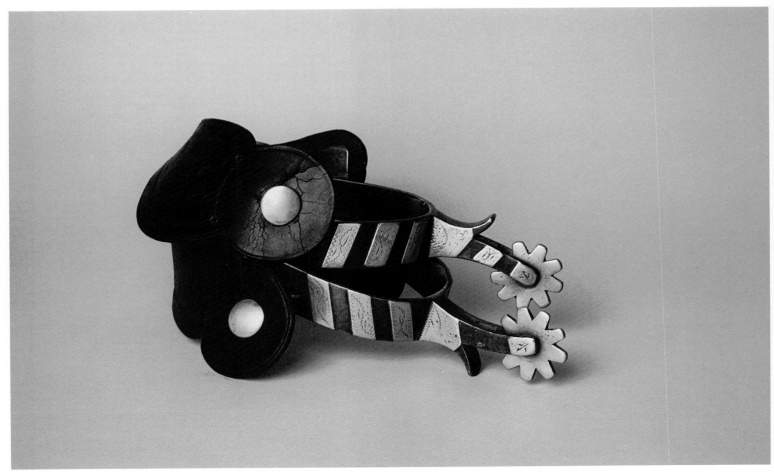

Pair of Texas style silver overlay spurs. Circa 1910. Marked O. Crockett in heel band. Collection: Joe Gish.

Large, single mounted spurs, circa early 1900s, made by Crockett of Kansas City, Missouri. "Crockett" (next to the oldest Crockett marking) is stamped on the underside where the heel band joins the shank. Collection: Vic Williams.

Both nickel plated metal and leather heel bands are marked "Buermanns Patent" on these unusual spurs. The downturned shanks feature 2⅝" saw-toothed rowels with Roman numerals one through twelve stamped into them. The straps are floral carved with both leather and brass conchos, circa 1880s, made by the August Buermann Manufacturing Company of Newark, New Jersey. Buermann's Company manufactured 443 different spur styles between 1868 and 1926. Judging from the downturned shanks, heel chains, and early strap style, these spurs could date back to the trail-driving days. Collection: Douglas Deihl.

Texas style gal-leg spurs with upturned heel band and stationary buttons mounted on one side with engraved German silver. These spurs also feature basket-weave straps with nickel silver conchos marked "Crockett" under the buttons, circa late 1930s, made by the Crockett Bit and Spur Company of Lenexa, Kansas. Collection: Douglas Deihl.

Pair of Bianchi spurs made by Joe Bianchi of Victoria, Texas with the initials "F.E.G" engraved on the two large Mexican coins mounted on the spur straps. These spurs were special ordered for Fred Engles Graham of Victoria, Texas in the 1920s. Collection: Jim Holley.

Excellent double mounted full overlay "Booger Reds" with R. T. Frazier straps and 10 point rowels, made by O. Crockett, probably of Kansas City, Missouri and marked inside the band, circa 1918-1920. "Booger Red" was an old bronc rider after whom Crockett named one of his models; this was a common practice among spurmakers. Collection: Bill Adamson.

Randy Butters is one of the best of today's spurmakers, as this pair of silver overlay Swans will attest. This work compares favorably to that which was done in the "golden age" of spurs, circa 1980s. Collection: Michael Friedman.

These impressive spurs by Kelly Bros. feature oversized rowels and were probably special ordered, circa 1920s. Collection: Dick Engle.

A fine pair of lady's spurs in excellent condition with interesting heart-shaped button and suits of cards motif, circa 1930, made by Sam Bass, Tulia, Texas. Collection: C.W. Lyle, Jr.

The Spanish influence is most apparent in the California style spur which, in addition to silver inlay, often had *pajados*, or "jingle bobs," which were small metal drops suspended from the rowel pin. Jingle bobs were purely decorative and created a pleasant musical sound as the cowboy rode or walked along the wooden sidewalks of the Old West.

G.S. GARCIA

Born in Sonora, Mexico in 1864, Guadalupe S. Garcia moved to Margarita California as a young boy. In 1894 at the age of 30 he married and moved to Elko, Nevada. As an experienced saddlemaker, Garcia went on to become one of the legends in his field. His saddles, bits and spurs are among the most desirable and sought after of all makers and are of the highest quality. Garcia's work opitimizes the California style of spurmaking, utilizing elaborate silver inlaid designs. Often copied, his work stands among the very best. At the age of 69, Garcia died in 1933.

Exceptionally fine engraved and inlaid, early California style spurs in excellent condition, circa 1890 to 1920. These spurs once belonged to Charles Russell. Collection: Dick Engle.

Lots of times I have ridden around the herd, with lightning playing and thunder muttering in the distance, when the air was so full of electricity that I would see it flashing on the horns of the cattle, and there would be balls of it on the horse's ears and even on my mustache, little balls about the size of a pea. I suppose it was static electricity, the same as when you shake a blanket on a winter night in a dark room.

We Pointed Them North

Extraordinary, double mounted, silver inlaid early California spurs, circa 1900. Collection: High Noon.

Very fine pair of spurs by G.S. Garcia of Elko, Nevada, circa turn-of-the-century. Garcia Sombrero conchos are rare. Collection: C.W. Lyle, Jr.

August Buermann silver-inlaid spur No. 1418. Beautifully engraved with etched rowels, as fine as any California spur and probably made by a California craftsman, brought to New Jersey by the astute Buermann, circa 1910-1920. Collection: High Noon.

California spurs with original leathers and conchos made by Edward H. Bohlin, circa 1925, reputed to have belonged to the famous movie cowboy Hoot Gibson. Note the "G" at the center of the heel band. Collection: George Pitman.

Silver mounted California spurs, circa 1920s, with coin silver mounted on one side and engraved silver pattern on the other side. The leathers have deep hand carving and engraved silver conchos. The spurs were acquired in Santa Fe, New Mexico and reportedly were used in that area. Collection: Joe Gish.

Double mounted California spurs with 2½" rowels. The leathers are hand-carved with the maker's name, Peg Garcia of Santa Barbara. The conchos were made from old, silver, 1880s coins from Argentina and Chile. They were probably made sometime in the 1920s. Collection: Joe Gish.

An early, classic pair of California style spurs with engraved silver inlays and mounted domes on one side only. They feature 2½" rowels on extreme down turned shanks and double heel chains, circa 1890s. The fine workmanship and sculptural qualities, coupled with the early style down turned shanks, add to their appeal. Collection: Douglas Deihl.

Double-mounted silver inlaid/overlaid California style spurs by J. Figueroa of Los Angeles, California with 2¼" overlaid rowels and matching conchos. The majority of Figueroa's work was unmarked, circa 1920s to 1930s. Collection: High Noon.

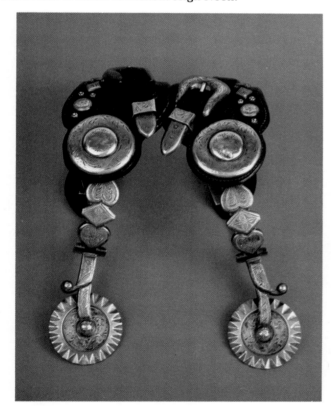

Beautiful pair of California spurs with silver engraved overlay on rowels made by Mike Morales, circa 1920. These spurs are visually exciting and distinctive. Collection: James Statler.

California silver inlaid spurs with Edward H. Bohlin straps, rowels and rowel insets, an interesting combination of *vaquero* and Tom Mix style, circa 1930s. Collection: High Noon.

Spurs by G. S. Garcia of Elko, Nevada, marked "Dandy No. 75A". According to the 1903 Garcia reprint, "This is the finest spur that has ever been made." They are double mounted with 100 different silver inlaid pieces, 14 point inlaid 2¼" rowels, engraved silver rowel covers, and original conchos on Garcia straps. These spurs are also marked with an "F" indicating that they were probably made by Filo Gutierrez while he was employed by Garcia, circa 1905. This spur was so successful that it was copied by Buermann, Morales, and others. Collection: High Noon.

Very good iron work spurs with engraved silver-mounted bands and crescent moon shanks in excellent condition, made by G. S. Garcia of Elko, Nevada, circa 1900-1920. Collection: Dick Engle.

This unmarked pair of spurs was made in the Arizona Territorial prison in Yuma, Arizona Territory. Prior to the turn of the century, they were owned by A. Johns, president of the Arizona Senate and were purchased from his estate. Collection: Roger Baker.

California silver overlay spurs, circa 1920, made by Mike Morales. Collection: George Pitman.

Spurs made by Mike Morales of Los Angeles, California, circa 1920.
Collection: James Statler.

Spurs made by G. S. Garcia of Elko, Nevada, circa 1915. Collection:
James Statler.

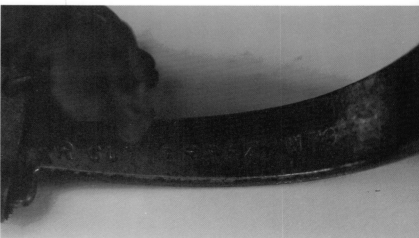

Spurs made by R. Gutierrez of San Francisco, California, circa 1915.
Raphael Filo Gutierrez was one of the finest of the California
spurmakers. He worked for G.S. Garcia as a young man and went
on to become well-known and respected in his own right. Collection:
James Statler.

Fine pair of double-mounted California spurs, inlaid and engraved on both sides, circa 1887-1889, made by J.F. Echavarria of San Jose, California. An advertisement for this type of spurs by Echavarria appeared in a Alturas, California brand book in 1887. Collection: George Pitman.

Fine quality workmanship characterizes G.S. Garcia spurs and bits. Excellent condition, circa 1900 to 1920. Collection: Roger Baker.

Silver mounted California spurs made by Visalia Stock Saddle Co., San Francisco, California, circa 1920. Collection: James Statler.

19th century, unmarked, California style silver inlaid spurs with fine and delicate engraving accented with a fine silver rope inlaid in rowel points and cast floral pattern conchos, circa 1870s. Collection: High Noon.

19th century, California style spurs attributed to Tapia. Fine rope inlay and exceptional iron work are complimented by four silver buttons. Collection: High Noon.

Unmarked pair of California spurs featuring engraved silver inlays on one side, single "jingle bobs", and early straps, circa 1900. Collection: Douglas Deihl.

Heart pattern spurs by G.S. Garcia of Elko, Nevada, this pair features Garcia's earliest mark, circa 1890. Collection: Roger Baker.

California silver mounted spurs, circa 1920, made by J. Figueroa of Los Angeles, California. Collection: George Pitman.

Long shanked spurs with silver inlays on one side, slots for heel chains, and old rosette stamped straps. They are marked "Morales" on the inside of the heelbands, circa 1900. Mike Morales worked for G. S. Garcia before moving to Portland, Oregon. He usually signed his spurs with a squashed M trademark under the buttons, or with his full name on the inside of the heelband. Spurs by Morales are very desirable. Collection: Douglas Deihl.

Finely wrought pair of California spurs, circa 1900 to 1910. Collection: Roger Baker.

Main and Winchester of San Francisco was founded at the time of the Gold Rush and produced a full range of cowboy gear. These silver inlaid spurs are examples of their fine work, circa 1880. Collection: Roger Baker.

Beautiful long shank, California style, silver mounted spurs which are finely engraved and in excellent condition, circa 1920s to 1930s. Collection: High Noon.

Classic California style spurs with coin silver inlays on one side and basket weave leather straps, circa 1920s, made by G. S. Garcia of Elko, Nevada. Listed as No. 44 in Garcia's 1914 saddle catalog, these spurs feature the "oval" marking on the inside of the heel band. Collection: Douglas Deihl.

Double mounted, silver inlaid spurs custom made with the original owner's initials on the heart-shaped buttons. This spur does not appear in the Garcia catalog, but does grace the cover of Morales' catalog No. 5, leading one to conclude that it was made by Morales when he was working for Garcia before 1910. Collection: High Noon.

Beautiful turn of the century California spurs with fine iron work on the bands, made by J. Figueroa of Los Angeles, California, circa 1890 to 1920. Collection: Dick Engle.

Gold and silver overlay fancy parade spurs, circa 1940, made by Edward H Bohlin. These spurs were made for the movie actor Ewing Mitchell who played the sheriff on the television program "Sky King". Collection: George Pitman.

California parade spurs with 14k gold overlay, circa 1939, made by Edward H. Bohlin. These were a special order presentation gift as noted on an engraved plaque on the inside strap. Collection: George Pitman.

Fancy parade spurs, circa 1938, made by Edward H. Bohlin with original leathers and conchos. Collection: George Pitman.

E.H. BOHLIN

Edward H. Bohlin left his home in Orebro, Sweden at the age of fifteen and arrived in New York in the year 1910. He headed west to the legendary town of Miles City, Montana where his first job was rounding up over nine hundred horses. Miles City was considered at the time to be both the horsetrading capital of America as well as a major shipping hub for cattle which had been driven north from as far south as Texas. Bohlin always had a strong interest in art and even attended the Art Institute in Minneapolis for a short time. He learned the art of making jewelry and crafting leather and eventually opened his first saddle shop in Cody, Wyoming just across the street from Buffalo Bill's Irma Hotel. At the same time he continued to punch cattle and performed rope tricks in a travelling theatrical company.

In Los Angeles, while performing at the Pantages theatre, Eddie heard a loud voice call out, "hey kid! What do you want for the coat?" The fellow had spotted the Calfskin black, white, and tan coat Eddie had made for himself. "Thirty-five dollars" Eddie yelled back. That proved to be one of the most important sales Edward Bohlin would ever make, as the man in the audience turned out to be the Hollywood legend, Tom Mix. Mix encouraged Bohlin to stay on in Los Angeles and open a shop catering to the affluent local clientele and movie stars. Before long, Bohlin would in fact become the saddlemaker to the stars including Hopalong Cassidy, Roy Rogers, Gene Autry, Clayton Moore "The Lone Ranger" and many others. His spurs, buckles, saddles and tack were the finest money could buy and examples of his work are among the most desirable and collected of all 20th century makers. E.H. Bohlin retired in 1972 and died in 1980. (Information courtesy of George Pitman)

Fine and rare, unmarked, early California silver inlaid spurs which appeared in the L.D. Stone, Main & Winchester, Garcia & Visalia catalogs, but due to the fragile nature of the thin, unreinforced horizontal rope, few pairs have survived intact, circa 1895 to 1910. Collection: High Noon.

Mike Morales-made, silver inlaid, one-piece spurs with the distinctive Morales shank and trademark "M" stamped below the button, circa 1925. Collection: High Noon.

Unmarked California style silver mounted spurs attributed to Mike Morales of Portland, Oregon. Finely engraved oversized 2-piece silver conchos. Collection: High Noon.

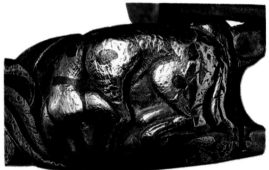

Mexican steel and silver spurs with an unusual sleeping dog motif. The original straps feature large heavy conchos. Collection: Enrique Guerra.

Open filigree work and sculptural scroll work give these early spurs a three dimensional effect. Gold inlays add to their appeal, circa 19th century. Collection: Roger Baker.

Fancy Mexican spurs of steel with silver mounts and conchos. Made for *coleaderas,* (a trick performed by turning a running bull off his feet by twisting the rider's leg around the bull's tail and throwing him.) They have small rowels and big conchos. The center of the rowels can be screwed out. These spurs are sometime called *coleaderas con antiojas.* Collection: Enrique Guerra.

Beautifully wrought Mexican steel spurs with silver birds and snakes intertwined with roses. These spurs are among the best of the period. Rare. Circa: 1870-1880. Collection: Enrique Guerra.

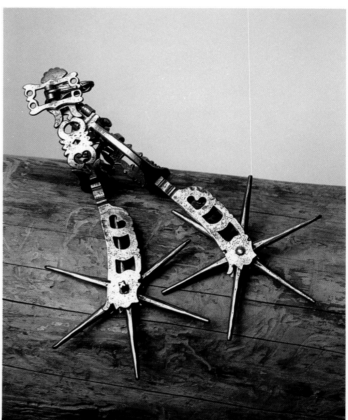

19th century colonial spurs made in Mexico following the Spanish Conquistador patterns. All steel, they are a good example of early Mexican spurs. Collection: Enrique Guerra.

Mexican silver mounted spurs with cookie cutter rowels. Silver inlay and intricate design distinguish these spurs, circa mid-1800s. Collection: Roger Baker.

Rare and magnificent middle-to-late-18th century Mexican colonial spurs which display the peak of the craftsman's art in silver mounted style with original leather straps and conchos. The straps are decorated with silver and gold thread embroidery. Collection: Enrique Guerra.

Mexican spurs in mint condition of silver on steel, circa 1890, with a design of intertwining coiled snakes on conchos. Leather straps are original with embroidered cactus fiber scorpions. Most of these spurs were custom made in the Amozoe Puebla. Collection: Enrique Guerra.

Rare Spanish colonial spurs with inlaid gold and open filigree work. Unique hand forged scroll design in the rowels, circa 1790 to 1820. Collection: Roger Baker.

Solid silver late Mexican colonial spurs. These fine examples show Spanish influenced large conchos. Circa 1830. Collection: Enrique Guerra.

Excellent quality Mexican double mounted snake spurs with silver mounting exhibiting two distinctly different patterns on each side, circa 1890. Collection: Roger Baker.

Mexican spurs, circa 1890, of silver with gold and copper inlays on steel. The snake eyes are made of green stones and gold thread is embroidered on straps in a pattern of intertwined snakes. Mint condition. Collection: Enrique Guerra.

Rare Mexican spurs of silver on steel, circa 1870. A very unusual motif of snails looking out from bands, all original and much used. Collection: Enrique Guerra.

An early pair of 21'' high cowboy boots with **Buermann** spurs made in the mid-1860s to 1870s. Left and right were indistinguishable in both military and cowboy boots of this period. The cowboy buying the boots would soak both feet (with the boots on) in water and keep them on for several days, thus forming the boots to each foot. These rare boots were found in New Mexico. Collection: Jim Holley.

Bench-made cowboy boots, in fine condition, circa 1890, from Omaha, Nebraska, 18'' tall with cloth pull straps marked "Kirkendall." The spurs are California silver mounted with coin silver conchos on straps. Collection: Joe Gish.

This 1880s cowboy boot was found in the basement of an old dry goods store in Brownsville, Texas. Never worn, the leather deteriorated from age. The spur is Mexican from same period as the boot with 3¾'' biscuit cutter rowels. Spurs like this were worn by South Texas cowboys. Collection: Joe Gish.

High-heeled boots weren't made for footwork and he wouldn't be caught in a low heeled shoe. But he didn't shirk any duty as long as it could be done from hossback. He worked without complaint long hours through flood and drought, heat and cold, dust and blizzard, never once thinkin' of his own discomfort if the cattle or the welfare of his boss demanded his attention.

The Old-Time Cowhand

Chapter Two

Boots

The evolution of the cowboy boot dates back to the time of the American Civil War. In fact, many boots from the 1860's are indistinguishable from those issued to the military. These boots were plain and utilitarian with low heels and squared-off toes. In early boots, it is impossible to determine the left foot boot from the right.

As time went by the cowboy boot became more and more distinctive. Because of their constant use on horseback, a reinforced arch and a higher, under-sloped heel evolved. This style of heel and the pointed toe not only made it easier to enter the srirrup and keep the foot securely in place, but also prevented the cowboy from getting hung up in the stirrup and possibly dragged after being thrown from a bucking horse. Thin leather soles enabled a surer fit in the stirrup.

Later, boots became more decorative with fancy stitching and long pulls known as "mule ears." Early mule ears were long, overhanging pieces of leather and are quite rare. Later, pulls were made of woven fabric and did not overhang the outside of the boot.

The height of a man's boot was usually determined by the type of topography he rode, but they were generally about 17" tall. Higher boots provided more protection. After the turn of the century, boots became more decorative with V-shaped tops, more elaborate and sometimes multi-colored leather and fancy stitching, and various heights. The side stitching on a boot is not purely decorative since it gives greater stability to the uppers and prevents wrinkling at the ankles. Beginning in the 1920's bootmakers made use of various colored leather pieces by stitching them together to form designs which were often quite elaborate and beautiful.

High-top riding boots, probably pre-1900 but possibly from the Civil War period. This type generally is seen in photographs of Civil War Cavalry Officers and Wild West show stars such as Buffalo Bill. Collection: Vic Williams.

Early cowboy boots with minimal stitched decoration on the uppers. These boots are transitional from the military/civilian style to the first real cowboy boots. There is no left or right which is characteristic of the earliest boots. Circa: 1870's. Collection: Michael Friedman.

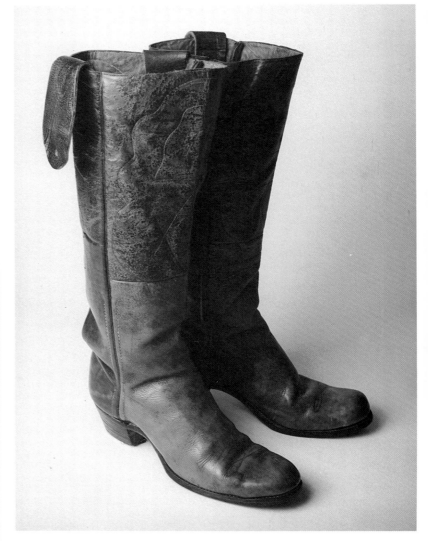

These "Muleys," or mule-ear boots, circa 1890, belonged to the famous Old West entertainer Texas Jack. Collection: C.W. Lyle Jr.

Black mule-ear boots, circa 1890s. Silver gal-leg spurs. Straps on the spurs are marked "Becker, Prantz, Ariz." Collection: Vic Williams.

Mule-ear boots, circa 1880s. Texas spurs with jingle bobs. Collection: C.W. Lyle, Jr.

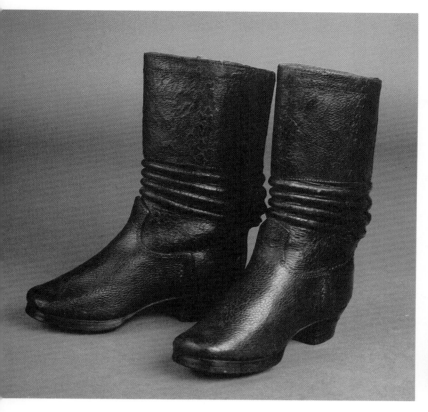

Very unusual childs boots with flexing "accordion" feature built in to the uppers. No left or right. Excellent condition. Circa: 1880. Collection: Michael Friedman

A pair of child's boots, circa 1850s, with square toes in excellent condition. Collection: Vic Williams.

Salesman's sample boots, circa 1850. Collection: Vic Williams.

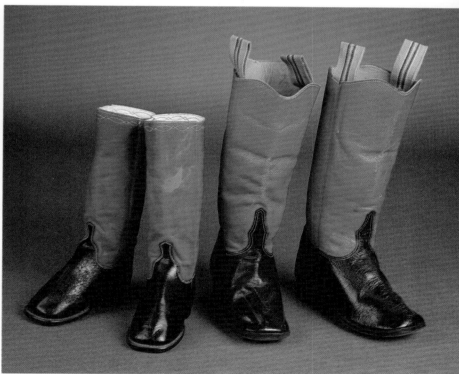

Two pairs of early boots in unused, original condition. The pair on the left are only 7'' tall and are probably a salesman's sample. Circa: 1860. Collection: Michael Friedman.

These boots illustrate just how exciting boots became by the late 1940s and '50s. The maker is unknown yet the skill displayed in the cutwork is exceptional. They are unique in their inlay/overlay construction and the realism of the figure. Collection: Mark Hooper.

Detail. Collection: Mark Hooper.

1940's boots by Abraham Rios showing his classic toe and heel covering in turtle or lizard hide. The decoration shows an American eagle holding an olive branch and arrows. Leuchese put Rios in charge of designing the statehouse series. Collection: Mark Hooper.

Well made 1940s boots, probably American. These low top boots are known among collectors as "pee-wees". Collection: Mark Hooper.

This pair of boots was made by G.C. Blucher of Olath, Kansas for Nay Cherry, one of the first black rodeo stars. They feature an alligator-skin chest on the eagle as well as personalized gold and silver heel and toe caps. Collection: Mark Hooper.

A pair of exceptionally fine boots. Probably made in the 1930s in the San Francisco area. The top lacing is uncommon. Collection: Mark Hooper.

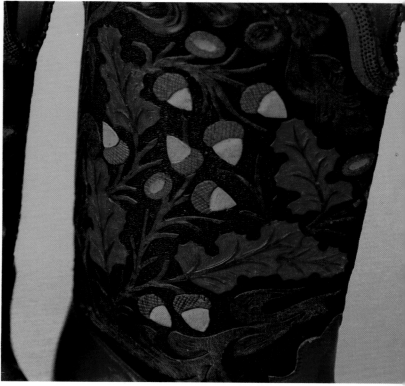

Detail. Collection: Mark Hooper.

Hand made boots by Hyer of Olath, Kansas with spurs made by Crockett, circa 1930s. Collection: C.W. Lyle, Jr.

Alligator boots made by Nacona with embossed silver and Bohlin-made spurs. Ex-collection Tom Mix and previously in the Hearst Museum in California. Collection: C.W. Lyle, Jr.

Handmade cowboy boots with hand-carved tops—leather pull tabs C.P. Shipley saddlery Kansas City, Missouri, made for R.F. Warren on August 20, 1923. Spurs are C.P. Shipley. Collection: Joe Gish.

These boots have fine hand carved floral design on the uppers and engraved sterling toes and heels. Circa: 1910. Collection: Michael Friedman.

Multi-color overlay ladies boots. Butterfly design. Circa 1920s. Collection: Michael Friedman.

A pair of boots by Tres Caballeros, a Mexican firm active in the 1950s and '60s. Showing a stovepipe or high top form. Collection: Mark Hooper.

A pair of 1940s boots by Stewart Romero of Los Angeles, a boot maker to the movie stars. These feature a unique floral design including pulls, double overlay on the leaves, and a textured effect on the flowers caused by stuffing cotton behind the petals prior to sewing. Collection: Mark Hooper.

1940's "puckered rose" boots by H.H. White of Fort Worth, Texas. These display some of the finest textured work. The unusual color scheme is distinctive. Collection: Mark Hooper.

Boots of unknown origin acquired in Albuquerque, N.M. They were probably constructed in Mexico, since it was popular in the 1940s and 1950s to tool one's own tops and take them to Mexico to be made up. Collection: Mark Hooper.

Fine pair of fancy boots with thunderbird overlays on the toes, circa 1930s to 40s. These multi-colored beauties even have the star of Texas. Collection: Roger Baker.

Multi-colored floral overlay cowboy boots. These boots required a great deal of work. Flat top. Circa 1950. Collection: Michael Friedman.

Rhinestone cowboy boots. This pair of 1950s or 60s boots, literally encrusted with rhinestones, were made for Robbie Robinson, lead guitarist for musicians Del Reeves and Bill Carlisle of the Grand ol' Opry. They were made in Alma, Arkansas and were worn on stage. They illustrate the extremes that boot designs reached during the period for entertainers affecting an Old West image. Collection: Mark Hooper.

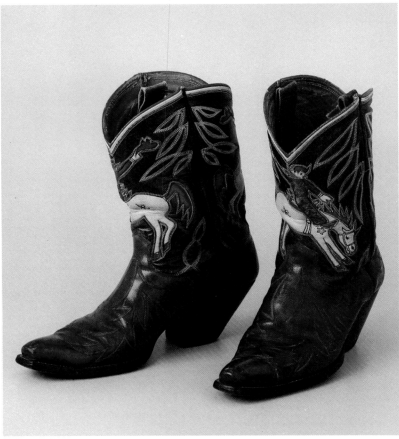

A pair of 1940s bucking bronco boots by Abraham Rios. Collection: Mark Hooper.

Detail showing the classic tongue and cutwork of Abraham Rios. These were made for a New Mexico rancher whose brand is on the horse. Collection: Mark Hooper.

Exceptionally well constructed boots from the 1930s with unusually fine design and cutwork. Floral pattern seems to flow with the form of the boot. The toe and heel foxing are perfect accents. Found in Southern California, they probably were made by a Mexican or American border maker. The design work has much in common with that of Abraham Rios, yet the tongue has a distinct form that is definitely not his. Collection: Mark Hooper.

Detail. Collection: Mark Hooper.

Boot Jacks

A cast iron boot jack, circa 1800s, in the "Double Star" design which is a different size on each end so it can be used by adults or children. Collection: Vic Williams.

A "Beatle"-style boot jack with rich original colors. Collection: C.W. Lyle, Jr.

The beatle bootjack is a common form. What sets this apart from the rest is the colorful, original paint, circa 1890. Collection: Michael Friedman.

Cast iron loop boot jack, circa 1880. Collection: C.W. Lyle, Jr.

Wooden boot jack belonging to the famous Wild West Show performer Buck Taylor. On the top are tacked the names of cities in which he performed, and on the bottom is painted "Buffalo Bill's Wild West" and "Pawnee Bill's Far East", circa 1890s. Collection: Michael Friedman.

Large, painted, wooden boot jack with heart cut-out, circa 1864. Collection: Michael Friedman.

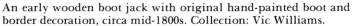

A cast iron boot jack, circa 1800s, in the "Cricket" style, but unusually large. In colonial times, a cricket on the hearth was believed to bring good luck. Collection: Vic Williams.

An early wooden boot jack with original hand-painted boot and border decoration, circa mid-1800s. Collection: Vic Williams.

A cast iron "Boss" boot jack, circa 1880s. Collection: C.W. Lyle, Jr.

A cast iron boot jack, circa 1800s, known as a "Naughty Nellie" with an unusual hair style. Collection: Vic Williams.

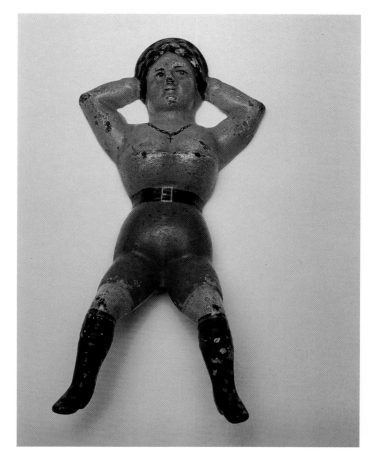

A "Naughty Nellie" boot jack in original paint, circa 1880s. Collection: C.W. Lyle, Jr.

A cast iron boot jack, circa 1800s, looks like a single-shot percussion pistol when folded. Collection: Vic Williams.

Chapter Three

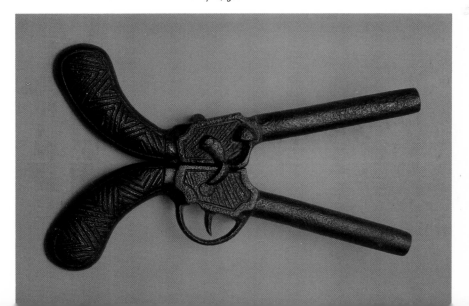

Hats

Montana peak cowboy hat with original hatband, circa early 1900s. Pencil roll brim. Maker: John B. Stetson. Collection: Michael Friedman.

The real cowhand's typical day was anything but romantic. There was no romance in gettin' up at four o'clock in the mornin', eatin' dust behind a trail herd, swimmin' muddy and turbulent rivers, nor in doctorin' screw worms, pullin' stupid cows from bog holes, sweatin' in the heat of summer and freezin' in the cold of winter.

The Old-Time Cowhand

A cowboy hat from the early 1900s, with a 5" brim with bound edge and a 7½" crown, marked in the sweatband "Prior, Denver." The purple satin lining has a cowboy and horse in the center marked "The Rancher." The old horsehair hatband was made by a cowboy on the McAllen ranch in Southern Texas. Collection: Joe Gish.

Stetson hat with large 5" brim and 6" crown. The expression 10 gallon hat would apply here. ✳ Collection: Michael Friedman.

A felt hat with a three-color braided horsehair hat band from the early 1920s. Labeled "Wolfes, Salt Lake City, Utah." [Hand engraved silver City Marshal's badge.] Collection: Vic Williams.

When you're ridin' the plains in the summer with the sun tryin' to soak all the tallow out of your spinal column, that old wide brim made it like ridin' in the shade of a cottonwood, and the high crown furnished a heap of space to keep the head cool. With it shadin' the eyes you could see long distances without gettin' sun blind when a lot depended on your vision. If the sun was on your back you could tilt that old John B. to cover the back of your neck for protection. The wide brim made a good shelter, too, when you was tryin' to snatch a little daylight sleep. In rainy weather it made a fine umbrella, keepin' the rain from runnin' in your eyes or down your neck. The crown made a handy water bucket. Many a grateful hoss has stuck his soft muzzle into a hat crown filled with water when he was unable to get water 'imself. He might use it for a water bucket to put out a fire when he broke camp, and more'n one hat has been used to beat out a grass fire before it got too much start. Fires were started with it too, by usin' it as a bellows to encourage a sickly blaze.

The Old-Time Cowhand

Black velour cowboy hat, circa 1910 to 1920, with a rolled edge on the 4" brim, red silk lining, and a braided horsehair hatband with silver decoration. Collection: Joe Gish.

Beige cowboy hat with a fancy silver mounted hat band. The finely engraved buckle has a gold bucking horse surrounded by 31 sterling conchos. Although unmarked, this is typical of work done in southern California for parade riders by such firms as Sunset Trials, Hollywood Saddlery, McCabe and Fredholm, circa 1930 to 1940. Collection: High Noon.

A white Stetson hat with a blue silk lining from 1910. The 4" brim and 7½" crown is marked in the sweatband with a gold Stetson logo, and on other side "Visalia Stock Saddle Co. San Francisco, Cal." It is hard to find old Stetsons with saddlery shop names in them. Collection: Joe Gish.

A fine old cowboy hat with a 7½" uncreased crown and 4½" brim, nickel spotted leather hat band marked in the sweatband "XXXX quality M. Hat Co." was worn by a cowboy on the John Dunn ranch in Nueces County, Texas in the early 1900s. Collection: Joe Gish.

This Stetson hat, with a 5½" brim, 7½" crown, and an old horsehair hatband was sold by a dry goods store in Abilene, Texas, circa 1900. Collection: Joe Gish.

Early, extra-wide brim cowboy hat referred to as a "Plainsman's hat." Collection: Vic Williams.

A Stetson labeled "Al Furstnow, Miles City, Montana" who was in business from 1884 to the early 1930s, this hat circa 1920s. Collection: Vic Williams.

Cowgirl hat made of Nutria fur. This extraordinary hat was a presentation to the winner of the World's Champion Ladies Bronco Competition in Cheyenne, Wyoming. Maker: John B. Stetson. Collection: Michael Friedman.

This high quality Stetson hat with a 5½" brim has an old nickel spotted leather band, circa 1900. Collection: Joe Gish.

A felt western hat from the early 1900s made by Chas. P. Shipley, Kansas City, Mo. who was in business from 1885 to 1967. Collection: Vic Williams.

Sombreros

Early and extremely rare Mexican hat, circa 1860, with a low crown, large brim, and gold and silver hat band. Collection: Enrique Guerra.

Early Mexican sombrero with gold thread embellishments. This low crowned hat is of the early period and quite rare. Circa 1860. Fine condition. Collection: Michael Friedman.

A Mexican hat, circa 1910 with gold thread embroidery made by Casa Tardon, Mexico City. Collection: Enrique Guerra.

Mexican sombrero, circa 1890—1910, with a very elegant silk embroidered monogram, probably made as a special order. While the common *vaquero* wore straw, these hats were only for the owners of large Haciendas. Most were made in Mexico city of fine felt or leather. Collection: Enrique Guerra.

Late period (circa 1900) heavy beaver hat with gold thread trim. Collection: Enrique Guerra.

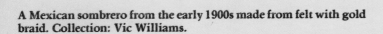

A Mexican sombrero from the early 1900s made from felt with gold braid. Collection: Vic Williams.

Salesman's sample sombrero with it's original hat box. Only 7" in diameter and 2½" tall, this silver braided little beauty is a rarity. Circa: 1880. Collection: Michael Friedman.

Beaver skin Mexican sombrero with large brim and crown, and silver and gold thread borders. This type of sombrero was worn only by the very wealthy. Circa 1870. Collection: Enrique Guerra.

A Mexican sombrero from the late 1800s made from heavy felt with gold and silver embroidery. Collection: Vic Williams.

A Mexican sombrero, from the 1880s to 1890s with gold and silver trim. Collection: Enrique Guerra.

Elaborately decorated Mexican sombrero. Circa early twentieth century, and in excellent condition. Collection: Michael Friedman.

Chapter Four

Cuffs & Gloves

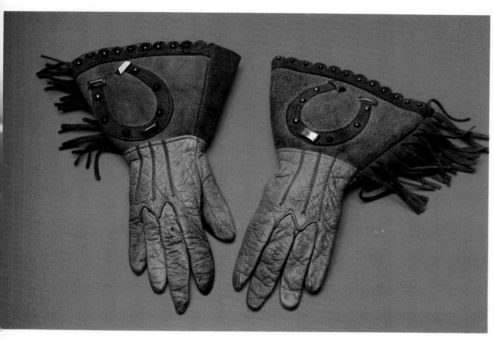

Cowboy gauntlets of an interesting design and construction, early 1900's. Collection: Vic Williams.

Fringed cowboy gauntlets with horseshoe design, circa 1900. Collection: Michael Friedman.

Leather cowboy gloves with fringe and an embroiderd star and border on the upper part of each glove, circa 1900. These are typical of the gloves cowboys wore when working out on the range; the ''Texas Star'' was a popular decoration. Collection: Jim Holley.

They were out there for months on end, on the trail or living in some cow camp, eating bad food, sleeping in wet clothes, going without everything that means life to a man-thought that was all they ever talked or thought about-and when they hit the bright lights of some little cow town that looked like gay Paree to them, they just went crazy.

We Pointed Them North

Beaded gauntlets with 9½'' cuffs worn by a performer in the 101 Ranch show in 1917. Collection: Joe Gish.

Cowboy fringed and beaded gauntlets, a fine example of a cross-cultural piece made for a white man but beaded by Plains Indians. Notice the unusual spot-stitched beads on the horses with saddles. Most Indian representations of horses are shown without saddles, circa 1890. Collection: Michael Garlenski.

Smoke-tanned elkskin gauntlets from the turn of the century. Collection: Vic Williams.

A small pair of early cowboy cuffs beaded on the top and bottom with one row of multi-colored beadwork, circa 1890. Many Indians became working cowboys after their removal to reservations. Most bead-decorated cowboy gear seems to have been made by the Western Sioux. These cuffs are unusual in their design, the colors and layout are more reminiscent of the Southern Plains Indians, and in particular the Kiowa. Collection: Douglas Deihl.

Nice pair of Indian beaded cowboy cuffs, circa 1895-1900. Sioux or Cheyenne. Collection: Jack Ringwalt.

Indian-made cowboy cuffs. Cross cultural pieces such as this are scarce. Circa 1900. Collection: Michael Friedman.

By 1880 Texas cattle had got as far north as Miles City, Montana and Texas cowboys with them. The name cowpuncher came in about this time, when they got to shipping a lot of cattle on the railroad. Men would go along the train with a prod pole and punch up cattle that got down in the cars, and that was how it began. It caught on, and we were all cowpunchers on the northern range, till the close of range work.

We Pointed Them North

Extremely decorative cowboy cuffs with conchos and spots. Horshoe design. May have been used by a Wild West Show cowboy. Circa 1910. Collection: Michael Friedman.

A fancy pair of cowboy cuffs made from two different style cuffs and heavily embellished with nickel plated brass spots. Circa 1920s. Collection: Douglas Deihl.

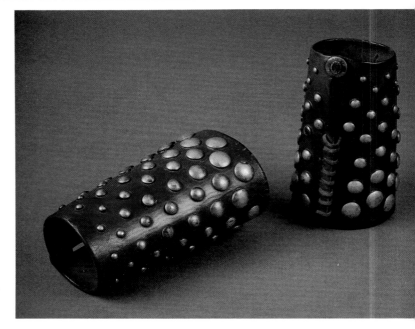

Interesting pair of Heiser cuffs with brass spots descending in size from top to bottom. Collection: Michael Friedman.

Left: Cowboy wrist cuffs which have seen a lot of hard use. Still in fine condition with many nickel plated brass spots, they are secured at the top with two rivets and have a buckle and a strap at the bottom of the cuff, 6¾'' high, made by D.F. Koke of Malta, Montana. Right: Very unusual pair of 1890s cowboy cuffs, 7'' high with scalloped tops and a large nickel spot in each flower center. Small, oval maker's stamp is at the top. Made by Dave Shelley of Cody, Wyoming. Shelly's shop made items for Buffalo Bill Cody. Collection: Joe Gish.

Fancy cuffs, circa 1920, made by Visalia Stock Saddle Company, San Francisco, California. Collection: George Pitman.

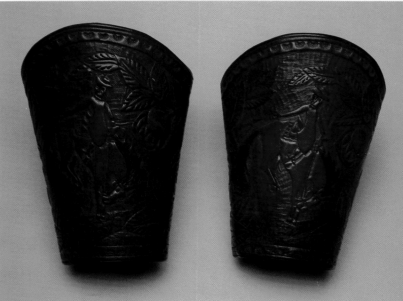

Fully carved cowboy cuffs featuring floral patterns and leather lacing on the back and bucking bronco riders on the front, circa 1920's. Collection: Douglas Deihl.

Fancy cowboy cuffs with red, white and blue enammeled studs. 7'' tall. Circa 1920s. Collection: Dominick Cervone.

Chapter Five

Chaps

Fine pair of "shotgun" chaps of excellent quality and condition, circa 1880s to 1890s. Collection: Jack Ringwalt.

Pair of buck stitched, fringed shotgun chaps, circa 1880 to 1890, made by F.A. Meanea. This is a fine pair of chaps, in excellent condition, and made by one of the best saddlemakers. Collection: Ken Bartlett.

Early pair of shotgun chaps, circa 1880s. Made by F.A. Meanea of Cheyenne, Wyoming. The earliest style of chaps from Menea's shop, they sold for $10 at the time. Collection: Joe Gish.

Shotgun chaps, circa 1890s to 1900, made by Tennison Bros. Saddlery of Dallas, Texas. Collection: Vic Williams.

These rare Mexican leggings are the precursors to chaps. Very few are known to exist. Collection: Enrique Guerra.

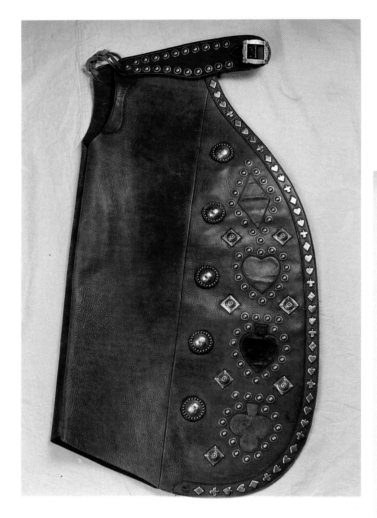

Fancy, unmarked, silver-mounted, batwing chaps with card suits motif and over 200 sterling conchos, probably made in Southern California in the 1930s. Collection: High Noon.

Fancy, hand-carved, siver-mounted dress chaps, circa 1940, made by Bob Brown with a McCabe silver buckle and conchos. During the golden age of the Western movies, Brown made much of the leather for the Hollywood cowboys including John Wayne, Roy Rogers, Gary Cooper and Hopalong Cassidy. He also designed much of the silver for the famed "McCabe Silversmiths." This pair of chaps represents the best of the craftsman's art in terms of the Hollywood cowboy period. Incredible as it sounds, Brown did all his carving with a screwdriver. He is still alive and lives in Big Bear, California. His work is represented at the Gene Autry Western Heritage Museum in Los Angeles, California. Collection: High Noon.

Chaps, cuffs and spurs by noted Hollywood maker Fred Fredholm, one of Bohlin's premiere silver workers. Sets such as this are scarce, circa 1930s to 1940s. Collection: High Noon.

Child's "shotgun" chaps with carved belt and pockets, spagetti fringe, and brass conchos. Fine patina. Made around the turn of the century. Collection: Michael Friedman.

Batwing chaps featuring 29 conchos, buck stitching and hundreds of nickel plated studs made by Visalia Stock Saddle Co. and stamped in three places on the belt, circa 1916. Collection: Douglas Deihl.

Fancy chaps, circa 1920, made by Visalia Stock Saddle Company, San Francisco, California. Collection: George Pitman.

Extraordinary pair of cowboy chaps. Made in 1912 by Hamley, these chaps possess almost every desirable motif element. White angora woolies with orange spots, bat wings with card suits, tacks, carved belt, and even the stars and the moon. Collection: Michael Friedman.

Pair of orange and spotted black Angora woolies. Made by Hamley of Pendleton, Oregon, circa 1910. Collection: Marvin Pruitt.

Pair of bright red Angora woolies, used in the 101 Ranch Wild West Show, circa 1930. Very unusual in this color. Collection: Marvin Pruitt.

Fine, two-color woolie chaps with carved belt and nickel plated conchos, circa 1920s, made by Visalia Stock Saddle Co. of San Francisco, California. Collection: High Noon.

Angora batwing spotted chaps, which were worn by Carl Romig, a cowboy and Wild West show performer who was with the 101 Ranch show in 1917. They were made by R.T. Frazier, Pueblo, Colorado. Collection: Joe Gish.

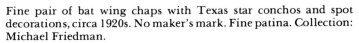

Fine pair of bat wing chaps with Texas star conchos and spot decorations, circa 1920s. No maker's mark. Fine patina. Collection: Michael Friedman.

Fancy batwing chaps worn by Tex McCloud who was with Tom Mix and performed with Buffalo Bill's Wild West show. Collection: Ken Bartlett.

Batwing chaps with circled star conchos, and a basket weave belt, circa 1920 to 1930, made by Heiser of Denver, Colorado. Collection: Jerard Paul Jordan.

Batwing chaps with six studded large stars on each leg and studded pockets, circa 1920 to 1930. They are said to have belonged to Hoot Gibson. Collection: Jerard Paul Jordan.

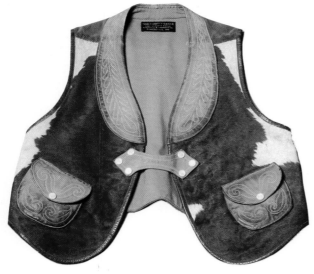

Batwing chaps and matching vest, circa 1900, made by C.P. Shipley of Kansas City, Missouri with fancy decorative stitching and mother-of-pearl buttons. Shipley was in business from 1885 to 1967. Collection: Vic WIlliams.

A pair of fancy, old batwing chaps in the classic style of Miles City Saddlery. The 1924 catalog shows them as #20 Chaparjos. They have a stamped drop belt, wide batwings, are mounted with 16 solid nickel plated conchos and 700 German Silver spots. They weigh 10 pounds and cost $27.00 when new. They are in fine condition showing use, but not abuse. The card suits were a favorite design among cowboys. Collection: Joe Gish.

Batwing chaps with Texas star as well as Texas spelled out in brass spots on the wings, made by E.B. Elam of San Antonio, Texas, they are said to have been worn by a silent movie cowboy in the 1920s. Collection: Joe Gish.

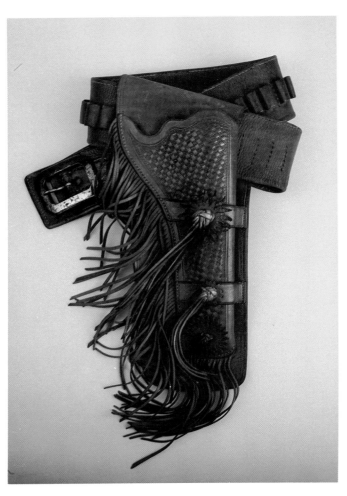

Ornate money/cartridge belt with long fringed holster, circa 1900. Collection: Michael Friedman.

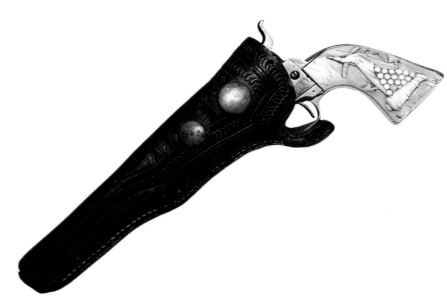

A well-worn slim-Jim style holster for a Colt 1851 Navy most likely made in the South during the Civil War period. The carved grip motif is very rare. Collection: Enrique Guerra.

Beaded Apache or Kiowa holster circa 1895-1900. Although beaded on a white man's holster, this piece was probably made by an Indian for an Indian. It is rare to find a figural representation such as the Thunderbird depicted here. Collection: Michael Friedman.

Signed S.D. Myres, El Paso, Texas, this "jock strap" holster accommodates a 7½" Colt single action; combined with a signed combination money/cartridge belt this is an impressive rig. Myres was responsible for the jock-strap design which added strength to the previous Mexican, loop-designed holsters. Collection: Thomas W. Connally.

1862 Colt Police pistol and an 1864 French intervention period, Mexican, military-style holster 6" long. The black leather has silver thread embroidery as crossed sabres and roses. Collection: Enrique Guerra.

Chapter Six

Gunleather/Holsters

Perhaps the one thing harder to find than a great old sixshooter is a great holster and gunbelt to house it. Far more perishable than the guns they held, frontier gunleather has become extremely hard to find, especially when it contains a cartouche bearing the name of the maker. By consulting records of where and when these saddle shops were in business, the approximate age of a piece can be calculated.

The evolution of the Western holster can be traced back to the early "pommel holster." Designed to fit over the pommel or horn on a saddle, these holsters were originally intended for use by the military. The same can be said for other early examples of holsters worn around the waist. Until Colt introduced the model 1851 Navy, the holster remained almost exclusively in the military domain.

With the Gold Rush and the subsequent settling of the West, saddle shops began to produce holsters and gunbelts for civilians. In the beginning, the designs were basically the same as those used by the military. Two civilian styles developed: the early "California" style, and the later "Mexican Loop" style. The "California" (or "slim-Jim" as they were often referred to) were shaped to fit the contour of the gun they held, usually the Colt percussion 1851 Navy. Some were perfectly plain while others had border stamping or floral carving. Some were made to be worn on the right side, but many of that early period were made for the left side, intended not for left-handed people but for the cross-draw. Very few civilian holsters retained a top flap, preferred by the military to protect and contain their pistols.

The advent of the Colt Single Action Army revolver in 1873 ushered in the most popular and collected style, the "Mexican Loop". Since the Colt S.A.A. or Peacemaker is considered the gun that won the West, it is the most sought after gun. So, too, are the holsters that were made for them; these are most often, although not always, of the "Mexican Loop" style. While made from only one piece of leather, this style of holster has two distinct parts, the skirt and the pouch. Slits cut into the skirt form loops to accomodate and secure the pouch (which holds the gun). Countless variations of this style include the number of loops, the contour of the top curve, construction and decoration. The basic form stayed intact throughout the remainder of the 19th century and into the 20th. Not until the period of the Hollywood cowboy was there a significant new variation, the Buscadero holster.

Slim-Jim holster for a Colt 1851 Navy shown here with a Navy square back model with ivory grips. Collection: Dr. James Brown.

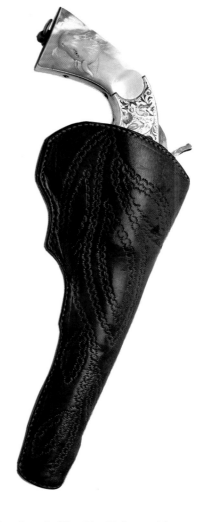

California style holster with hand-stamped border design for a Colt 1860 Army revolver, circa 1860s, made by Schalten and McAdams of Springfield, Missouri. Collection: Vic Williams.

Slim-Jim for an 1851 Navy with elaborate design, and very fine Mexican eagle ivory grips. Collection: Enrique Guerra.

California style Slim Jim Holster with hand-carved decoration—Gun is a factory engraved .44 cal. Merwin Hulbert with carved mother-of-pearl grips. Circa 1876—1880. Collection: Vic Williams.

A finely carved slim-Jim holster for an 1851 Navy Colt with an unsual form-fitting top on the holster. Collection: Dr. James Brown.

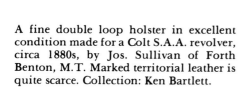

A fine double loop holster in excellent condition made for a Colt S.A.A. revolver, circa 1880s, by Jos. Sullivan of Forth Benton, M.T. Marked territorial leather is quite scarce. Collection: Ken Bartlett.

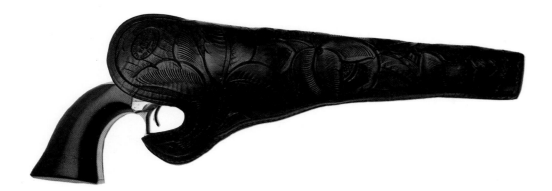

A Colt, 2nd Model Dragoon revolver which was in production only from 1850-1851. The holster of exceptional condition is hand carved in the California style and was made by Main and Winchester of San Francisco, California, who were in business from 1849 to 1905. Collection: Vic Williams.

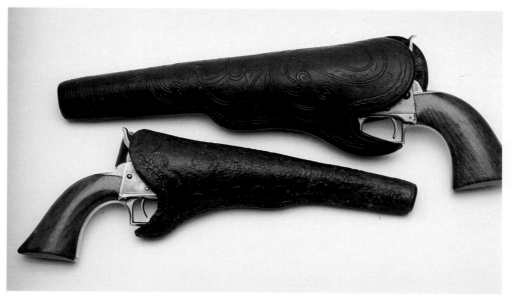

California-style floral pattern, left-handed holster with an "S"-curved pouch and toe plug for a 7½" Colt S.A.A. Collection: Dominick Cervone.

Top: Carved California-style holster for a 1851 Colt Navy, circa 1850s to 1860s. Bottom: Stamped California style holster for a Colt 1848 Baby Dragoon revolver, circa 1850. Collection: Vic Williams.

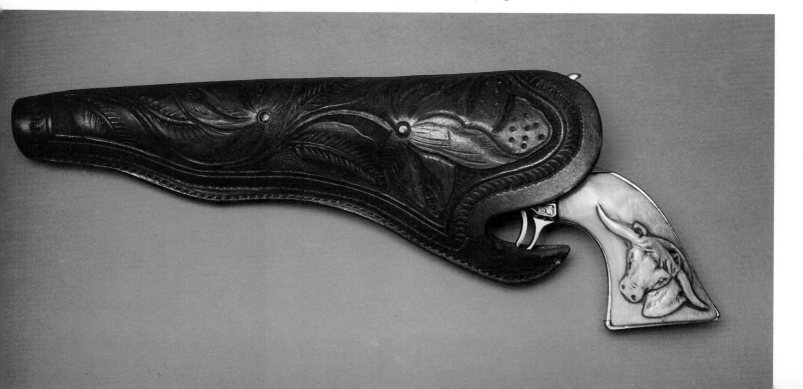

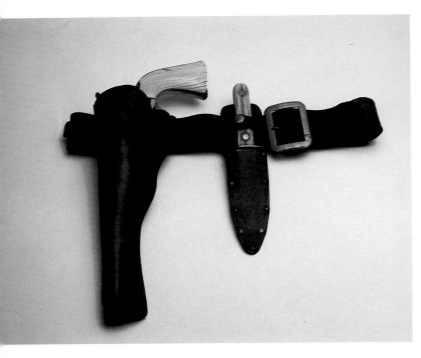

Slim-Jim holster with an 1860 Colt Army Conversion. The holster was made in the late 1870's or early 1880's by G. H. Tips from Houston, Texas. A Texas marked holster for a Conversion is rare. Collection: Jim Holley.

Short-skirted holster for a 7½" Colt single-action revolver, circa 1880 or earlier, made by N. Porter, of Taylorsville, Texas. When Taylorsville burned to the ground in 1880, N. Porter's business was moved to Abeline, Texas. When rebuilt, the town changed its name to Taylor, Texas. Collection: Jim Holley.

Slim-Jim holster for a 3rd model Dragoon pictured with a shoulder stock on page 145. Both the holster and gun were purchased directly from a Texas family. Collection: Dr. James Brown.

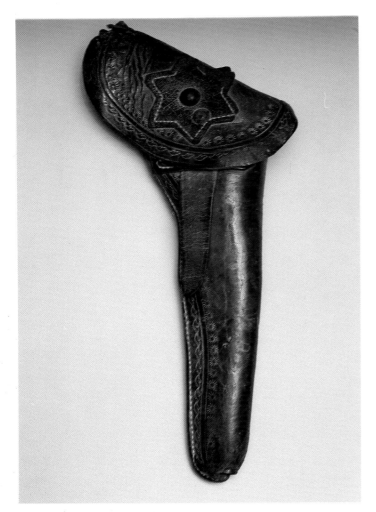

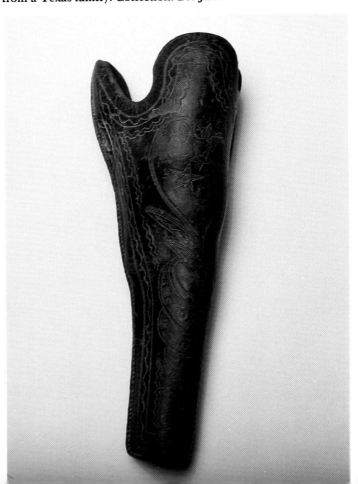

Texas-made holster with a Colt 1860 Army gun. This early civilian holster retains a top flap, typical of military holsters. Collection: Enrique Guerra.

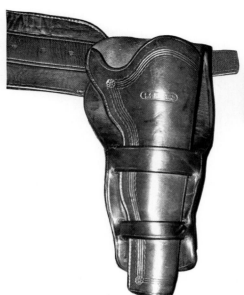

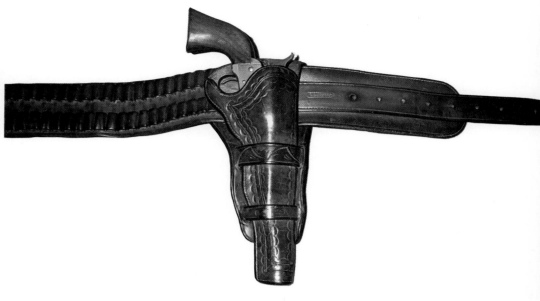

A beautiful and rare double-loop money and cartridge belt and holster, made to fit a Colt S.A.A. 7½'' bbl., with wonderful patina and border design, circa 1880s, made by F.A. Meanea of Cheyenne, Wyo. This is a classic rig from the Old West. Collection: Ken Bartlett.

A double-loop holster made by F.A. Meanea of Cheyenne, Wyo., circa 1880s which was made to fit a Colt S.A.A. 7½'' bbl. Collection: Ken Bartlett.

Three-loop holster and a cartridge and money belt marked ''R.T. Frazier, Pueblo, Colorado.'' Belt has 61 loops for .44 cal. cartridges. Collection: Vic Williams.

Extraordinary gun rig from the early period, circa 1885, made by E. Goettlich of Miles City, M.T. This rig was discovered packed away in an attic in Maine. It is truly a great example of a classic old holster and gunbelt. Among its desirable features are its pristine condition, the Territorial marking from an important Old Western city, its intent to hold a Colt S.A.A. 7'' bbl., and the belt's combination cartridge/money design. For the advanced collector, it doesn't get much better than this. Collection: Ken Bartlett.

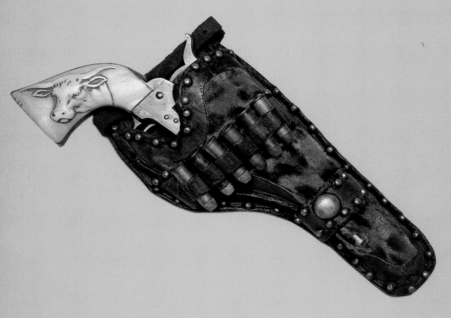

Holster for a colt S.A.A. made from ocelot skin with brass spots.
Collection: C. W. Lyle, Jr.

Holster for 4¾" Colt S.A.A. Marked S.C. Gallup, Pueblo
Colorado. Collection: Joe Gish.

A Colt revolver, 7½" barrel, .32 cal. made in the 1930s
with a carved American eagle on the pearl grips.
Collection: C. W. Lyle, Jr.

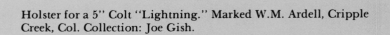

Holster for a 5" Colt "Lightning." Marked W.M. Ardell, Cripple
Creek, Col. Collection: Joe Gish.

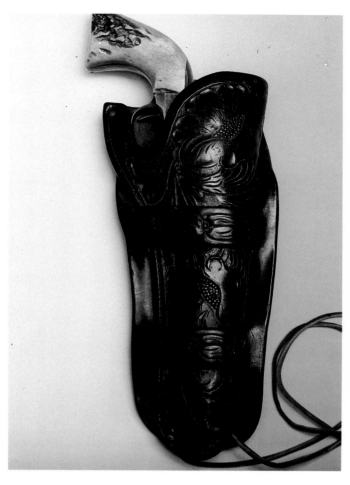

A single-action holster, circa 1900, featuring floral carving, stamped edging, and a sewn-in "Cheyenne" plug at the end of the pouch. This plain, early-style cartridge belt, circa 1870s, once belonged to Buffalo Bill Cody. Collection: Douglas Deihl.

Tooled leather holster, circa 1890s to 1900s, made by R.T. Frazier of Pueblo, Colorado. Collection: Enrique Guerra.

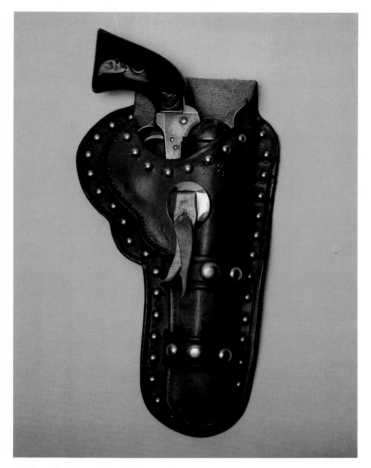

A double-looped, nickel-studded holster made to fit a 5½" Colt single-action revolver, circa 1910 to 1920. It has a contoured pouch and matching skirt edged with nickel spots. Collection: Douglas Deihl.

Basket weave single loop holster by S.C. Gallup of Pueblo Co., circa 1900-1920. The silver studs were probably added by a Navajo Indian as they are sinew sewn. Collection: Doug Deihl.

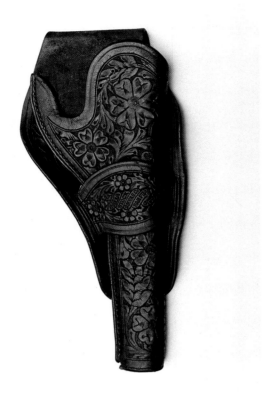

Single-loop carved holster for a 7½'' Colt S.A.A., made by Visalia Stock Saddle Company of San Francisco, California. Collection: Michael Friedman.

A two-loop holster for a Colt S.A.A 7½'' barrel, circa 1900, made by S.C. Gallup of Pueblo, Colorado with a rolled stamped border design. Gallup was in business between 1890 and 1928. Collection: Vic Williams.

It is unusual to find an early shoulder holster for a colt S.A.A., unmarked, circa 1890. Collection: John Kubicki.

Short-skirted holster for a 7½'' Colt S.A.A., circa 1870s to 1880s, made by H. C. Heilig of Castroville, Texas. This is an excellent example of an early Texas holster. The short skirt was typical of Texas holsters in the 1870s and early 1880s. Note the two Texas stars on either side of the maker's cartouche. Collection: Jim Holley.

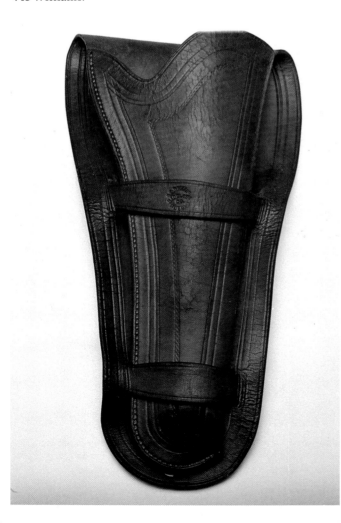

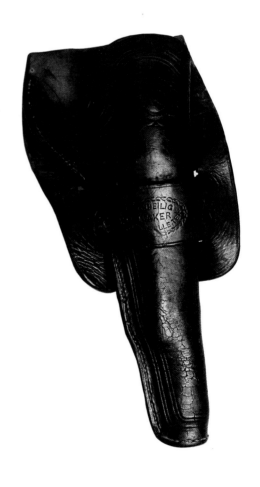

Early 1900s rig for a Colt .45, 4¾" S.A.A. The holster is nicely hand tooled with initials "B.W." and maker's stamp on the loop "H.P.C. Evers, Brady, Texas." The cartridge belt is two inches wide. Collection: Joe Gish.

A matching rig made by "H. H. Heiser, Denver, Colorado," circa 1910 to 1920. The holster, for a 7½" Colt S.A.A., has unusual triple loops. The belt is 4½" wide with shell loops for a .45 cal. pistol and rifle shells. Collection: Joe Gish.

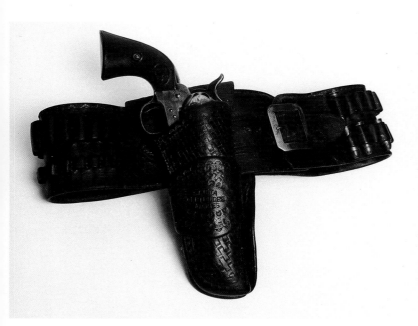

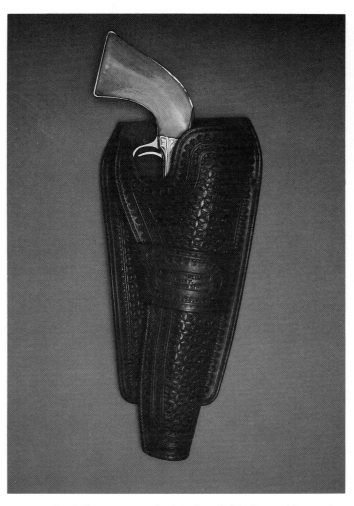

A holster for a 5½", single-action pistol, made before 1918 and marked "Santa Gertrudes Maker." A 3½" wide cartridge and money belt, circa 1918-1925, with a double row of .45 cal. cartridge loops marked "Kingsville Lumber Company. Running -W Brand, Kingsville, Texas." The King Ranch started its own saddle shop on the ranch in 1904 and stamped "Santa Gertrudes maker" on its saddles, holsters and belts. In 1918, the saddle shop was moved to the Kingsville Lumber Company building in Kingsville, Texas. Both marks are extremely hard to find. Collection: Jim Holley.

Montana single-loop, stamped, right-handed holster with toe plug made by William Wellman of White Sulpher Spings, for "Colt S.A.A. 7½". Collection: Dominick Cervone.

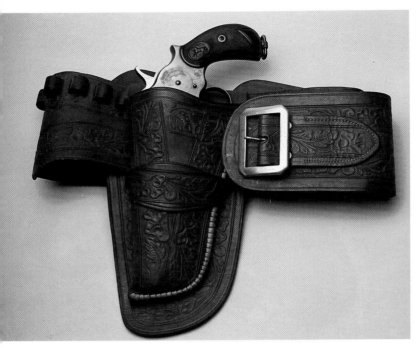

Holster and belt made by W. A. Harris of Tulsa, Oklahoma, with 28 loops for .44 cal. cartridges. In the holster is a Colt Model 1878 Double Action revolver with a 5½'' barrel. Collection: Vic Williams.

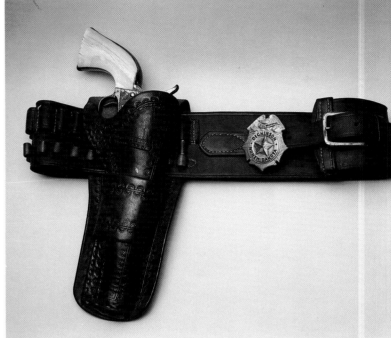

A fine and rare Old West lawman's rig including a 3½'' cartridge belt with loops for .45 cal. revolver, and rifle shells. The holster for a 7½'' Colt S.A.A. revolver features an attractive border design and is marked "Rattan Saddlery Co., Dickinson, N. D." The worn, one-piece badge with wire pin is marked "City Marshal, Dickinson, North Dakota" and has a maker's name on the reverse: "S.G. Adams, St. Louis". Collection: Joe Gish.

Colt third model Derringer also known as the "Thuer". Circa 1875. First type .41 caliber rimfire with varnished walnut grips in excellent original condition. Accompanied by a custom holster with engraved silver fittings. Collection: Vic Williams.

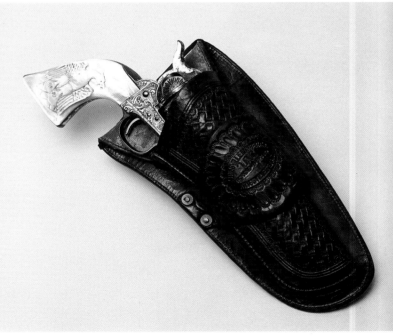

South Texas holster for a 5½'' Colt S.A.A. with a maker's stamp on the single loop reading "Kingsville Lumber Company. Running-W-Brand Kingsville, Texas." This company was owned by the King Ranch. The holster has a single loop attached with four rivets, circa 1925. Collection: Joe Gish.

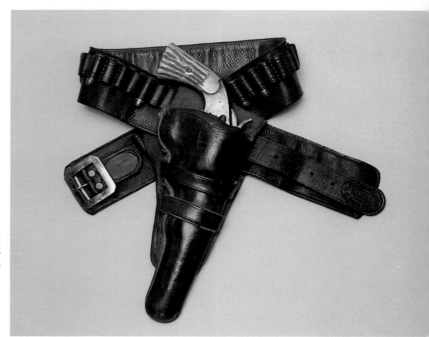

An early double-loop, Mexican style holster that fits a 7'' Merwin Hulbert, together with a combination money and cartridge belt made by the El Paso Saddlery Company. The holster dates circa 1880s, and the cartridge belt circa 1890s. Collection: Doug Deihl.

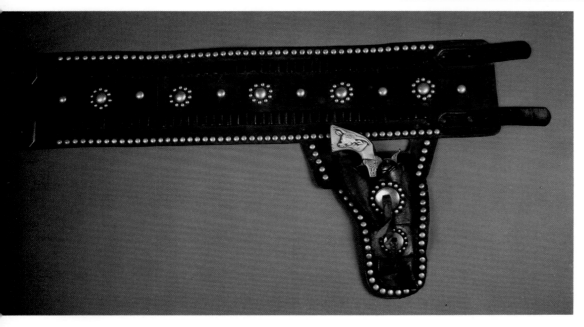

This ornately decorated buscadero rig was probably worn in a Wild West show, circa 1920s. Collection: Michael Friedman.

This Indian-made, fully beaded, single-loop holster and matching cartridge belt fit a 5½'' Colt single action revolver, circa 1900-1910. It was probably made by Sioux Indians of South Dakota. During the Reservation period, the Sioux had a tendancy to decorate many unusual items such as doctor's bags, holsters, cartridge belts, and even saddles with beadwork. This fully beaded matched rig was probably used on dress occasions, and is both colorful and rare. Collection: Douglas Deihl.

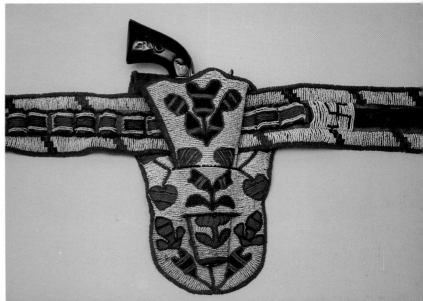

A fancy Buscadero rig of exceptional quality with buck-stitching and floral carving. The owner's initials are in nickel spots on both the belt and holster, circa 1930s to 1940, made by H.H. Heiser of Denver, Colorado. Collection: John Kubicki.

Indian-made, beaded and fringed pistol case, circa 1890 to 1900, made for a Colt, single-action revolver. Collection: Vic Williams.

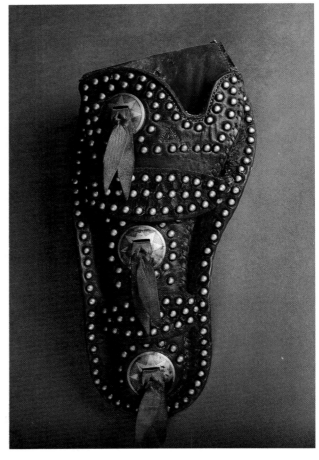

Heavily decorated and well worn double-loop holster for a Colt, single-action revolver, made by R.T. Frazier of Pueblo, Colorado. Collection: Michael Friedman.

Colt Newline .30 cal. rim-fire revolver in a rare singleloop leg holster (a hide-away), circa 1874-1876. Leg holsters are scarce. Collection: Vic Williams.

Rare wrist holster for a Remington over and under derringer, circa 1920s made by S. D. Myers of El Paso, Texas. Myers moved from Sweetwater, Texas, to El Paso, Texas, in 1920. Collection: Vic Williams.

But there is one thing I would like to get straight. I punched cows from '71 on, and I never yet saw a cowboy with two guns. I mean two six-shooters. Wild Bill carried two guns and so did some of those other city marshals, like Bat Masterson, but they were professional gunmen themselves, not cowpunchers. The others that carried two guns were Wes Hardin and Bill Longley and Clay Allison and them desperadoes. But a cowboy with two guns is all movie stuff, and so is this business of a gun on each hip. The kind of fellows that did carry two would carry one in the scabbard and a hide-out gun down under their arm.

We Pointed Them North

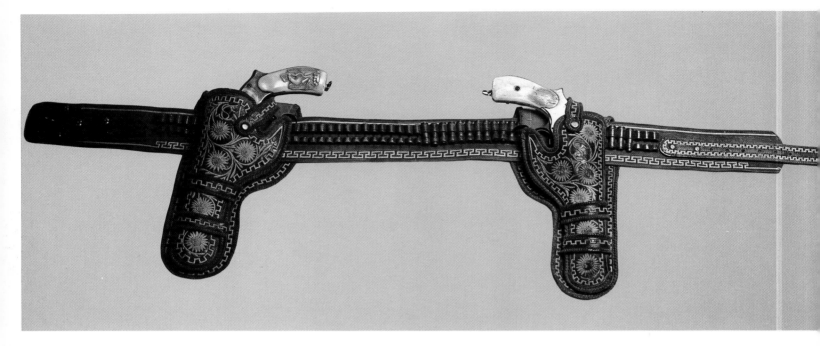

Made for Smith and Wesson revolvers, this Mexican double holster rig features cactus fiber embroidery; circa 1915. Collection: Enrique Guerra.

They were intensely loyal to the outfit they were working for and would fight to the death for it. They would follow their wagon boss through hell and never complain. I have seen them ride into camp after two days and nights on herd, lay down on their saddle blankets in the rain, and sleep like dead men, then get up laughing and joking about some good time they had had in Ogallala or Dodge City. Living that kind of life they were bound to be wild and brave. In fact there were only two things the old-time cowpuncher was afraid of, a decent woman and being set afoot.

We Pointed Them North

Early double-loop Mexican-made holster, circa 1870s to 1880s. A Colt .44, single-action, 7½'' with carved ivory grips is pictured in the holster. Collection: Enrique Guerra.

A Mexican cartridge belt for 7 mm rifle cartidges, circa early-1900s. The belt has 54 silver embroidered cartridge loops in the shape of bees. Collection: Vic Williams.

Opposite page:
Group of Mexican vaquero accoutrements. 19th century. Collection: Enrique Guerra.

Rare, signed "Main and Winchester" "Mother Hubbard" saddle. This extraordinary saddle was made in San Francisco during the Gold Rush. It's floral carved design is characteristic of M&W and it's exposed cantel and pommel relate to its vaquero influence. Stirrups are cut from a solid block of wood, circa 1850s. Photo: Steve Brown. Collection: Bob Hunn.

A very early and rare Texas saddle, circa 1830, with a silver-mounted horn and cantel that shows distinct Mexican influence. This saddle was probably made in Texas by a Mexican craftsman. The early horn saddlebags are in very fine condition. This type of saddle was used by horsemen during the Texas revolution of 1836. Collection: Enrique Guerra.

Chapter Seven

Saddles

If there were one item considered nearest and dearest to a cowboy, it had to be his saddle. He could survive without anything else, but his saddle was his most coveted possession. A working cowboy would spend upwards of a few months' wages to get a saddle just right for his needs and desires. Even a stock saddle, once broken in, was like an old pair of boots that conformed uniquely to it's owner's anatomy. It was, after all, the place from which he conducted his business and often the pillow upon which he rested his head. As with many other cowboy accoutrements, the first Western-style saddles appeared in Texas and California having evolved from Mexican saddles. It was easily distinguished from the English style saddle by its larger size and the presence of a horn which was essential for roping cattle. Stylistically, the western stock saddle developed regional characteristics, but in general these saddles were quite large, very comfortable and extremely durable. Most weighed about 35 pounds. Early saddles had a "slick" or "straight" fork located in the front of the saddle to which the horn is attached. As time went by, the slick fork evolved into a wider fork known as a "swell" fork. These swells made it more difficult for a rider to be thrown. The cantle, or back rest

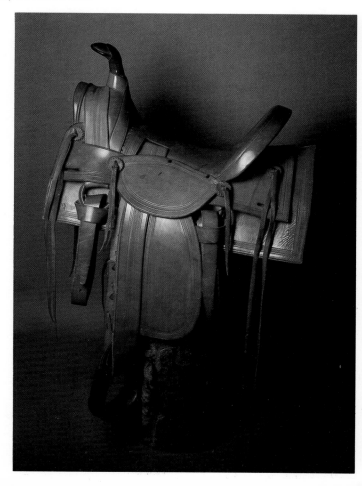

A saddle in mint condition, probably made for mail order house, circa 1880, it was found in an attic in Colorado. Collection: Enrique Guerra.

on a saddle, also varied greatly. A higher cantle was desirable in mountainous areas since it gave the rider a more secure seat as he climbed and descended steep inclines. Conversely, a low cantle made mounting and dismounting easier in the western flatlands. Other parts of the saddle also varied according to period and location. Distinctive characteristics of the skirt, rigging, stirrups and tapaderos could determine an individual's origin and in some cases what type of work he did. For example, the skirt on a California style saddle was round while a Texas style saddle would typically be square.

During the open-range period when there was no barbed wire separating one ranch from another, almost every community boasted a saddle shop. In nearly every cow town along the western cattle trails, a craftsman repaired or made saddles. Most shops passed into the history of the Old West with the same anonymity as the average cowpoke, but there were those whose talent and craftsmanship endured and whose work is still highly esteemed today. The following saddles are only a sampling of the range and uniqueness of the better saddlers. The names Gallatin, Meanea, Frazier and Visalia came to represent the best of the early period, while others (Bohlin, Meyers, and Keyston Bros.) continued the tradition and quality into the 20th century.

Unmarked Mother Hubbard saddle with rare apple horn. Texas, circa 1875. Collection: Dave Van Meter.

A fine and early Texas marked "Mother Hubbard" saddle made by R.F. Tackabery of Fort Worth, Texas, circa 1850s. It was owned by B.D.F. Pool. A trademark picture of a bull is on the fender. Collection: C.W. Lyle, Jr.

A classic "Great Plains" style saddle of the 1880s which features Sam Stagg double rigging with the back rings secured by the rear jockeys, and a Cheyenne roll cantle, circa 1885 to 1889. It was made by Robbins and Lenoir of Miles City, Montana. Although the strings have been replaced, this saddle is in beautiful condition for its age. The carved and stamped decoration is also very eleborate for this early period saddle. Collection: Douglas Deihl.

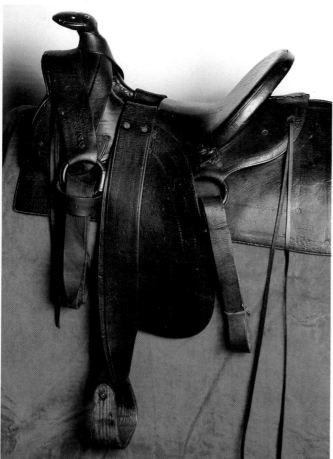

Very early Gallatin-style cowboy saddle from early 1880s, marked "#2, F.A. Meanea, Cheyenne, W.T." Made in the Wyoming Territory shortly after Meanea took over the shop from his uncle in 1879, it has seen lots of use, but is all there, ready to ride. Collection: Joe Gish.

California style saddle with elaborate border decoration. Excellent condition. Made in Oregon, circa 1890. Collection: Dave VanMeter.

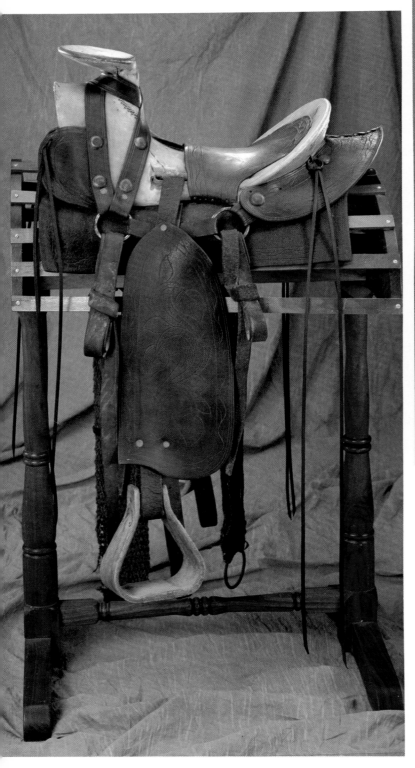

Rare, early "Hope" style saddle with large 6" diameter horn. Sam Stagg double rigged with cut tooled design. This all original unmarked saddle probably is from Texas and dates to the 1850-1870 period. Photo: Steve Brown. Collection: Bob Hunn.

This saddle is stamped in three places "G.H. & J.S. Collins, Omaha, Neb." In excellent condition, it has hand hammered conchos, a horse head horn cover, longhorn steer on the back of the seat, a moon, a shield, and a star on the stirrups, and a cantel rim. Reported to have been used by a cowboy in Buffalo Bill's Wild West show, it is an unusual and interesting saddle dating from the 1880s. Collection: Joe Gish.

An early Texas saddle of simple design with heavy Mexican influence, evidenced by the exposed tree, circa 1850. Collection: Enrique Guerra.

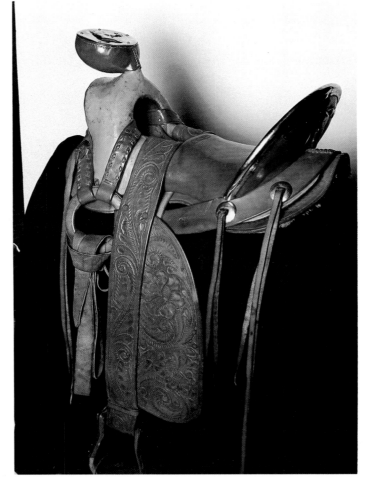

F.A. MEANEA

Frank A. Meanea was born in 1849 near Lexington, Missouri and began his career as a saddlemaker by repairing harnesses for the Union Pacific Railroad. In 1868, at the age of 19, he joined his uncle Ed Gallatin in Cheyenne, Wyoming where he was to become one of the major craftsmen in the history of the Western saddle. Gallatin himself is often referred to as the "Father of the Western Stock Saddle." The efforts of Meanea, Gallatin, and brothers Gilbert and John Collins resulted in what became known as the "Cheyenne Saddle." These saddles were so desirable that working cowboys were willing to spend as much as two months' salary and wait as long as it took to obtain one. An 1880 advertisement, shows Meanea saddles selling for $35.00 to $65.00. In addition to saddles, Meanea carried a full line of tack, bits, and spurs made by such distinguished names as Crockett, Kelly Brothers, and Buermann. While his saddles are highly sought after, his chaps, holsters, and gun belts are also considered extremely desirable among Western dealers and collectors. Frank Meanea bought out his uncle in the mid-1870s but the business retained the name E.L. Gallatin and Company, until 1881 when it became known as "F.A. Meanea." Throughout the 1880s and 1890s Meanea enjoyed great popularity, but as the open-range era of cattle ranching gave way to the approaching machine age, business slowly declined. At the age of 79, Frank A. Menea died in 1928.

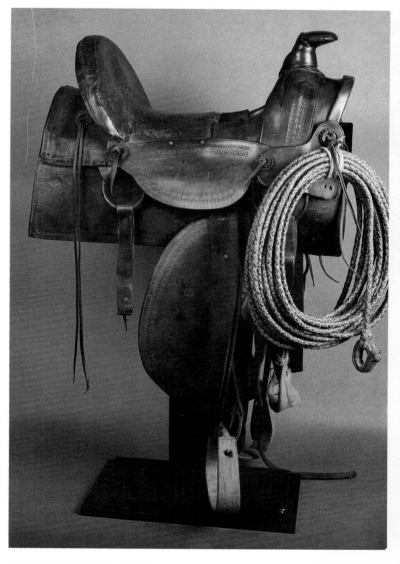

Early half-seat saddle with Sam Stagg rigging, circa 1880. Signed: C.W. Hess, Brenham Tex. Early Texas marked trail saddles are scarce. Probably because of the climate, most did not survive. Collection: Michael Friedman.

A classic half-seat "Cheyenne" style cowboy saddle in nice original condition. Made in the 1880's by E.L. Gallatin of Cheyenne, Wyoming Territory. Collection: Ken Bartlett.

Very fine saddle made by Main and Winchester of San Francisco, California. This circa 1880s half-seat saddle is fully carved and is an excellent example of an early California saddle. Collection: Ken Bartlett.

The old-time cowhand lived in the saddle. He was strictly a ridin' man, and detested walkin', even for short distances. A self-respectin' cowhand would never be caught goin' far on foot.

The Old-Time Cowhand

Half-seat territorial saddle with straight bound cantel. A classic cowboy saddle with Sam Stagg double rigging and sewn on side jockeys, made by J.S. Collins, Cheyenne, W.T. (Wyoming Territory). Listed in the catalog as #126, circa 1881-1885. Photo: Steve Brown. Collection: Bob Hunn.

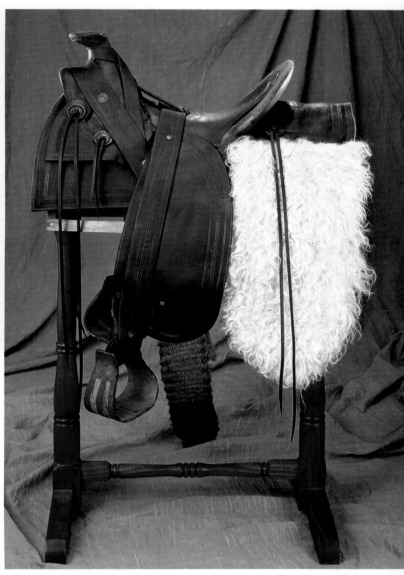

Early saddle marked G.E. Gray, Pendleton Or. Rawhide exposed cantel and Sam Stagg center-fire rigging with a very unusual leather brace running under the seat from cantel to horn. White angora serapes on rear. Wooden stirrups, circa 1860-1870. Photo: Steve Brown. Collection: Bob Hunn.

Main and Winchester

Among the earliest saddlers of the Old West was the company of Main and Winchester. Founded in San Francisco during the first year of the Gold Rush, Charlie Main and E.H. Winchester established what was to become one the premier saddlery business' of the period. Their reputation for quality was unquestioned and with close to 100,000 new arrivals to California in the year 1849, there was certainly a great need for their services.

Another pioneer San Francisco saddle maker was Lucius D. Stone, who in 1852 established the firm of L.D. Stone Co. In 1905 these two important makers consolidated to form Main-Winchester-Stone Co. offering a wide variety of items including bits, spurs, saddles, harness, hardware, chaps, etc. In 1912, after a long and successful carreer, they sold out to Keyston, one of the finest makers of 20th century parade saddles.

Today the marks of Main and Winchester, L.D. Stone, and Cowboy Brand (their consolidated trade mark) are highly prized by collectors.

Yellow-seat lady's saddle, circa 1919, Made by the Visalia Stock Saddle Co. and shown as #946 in the Visalia catalog. Collection: George Pitman.

A loopseat saddle that was found in a barn rolled up in a 50 gal steel drum. This maker was proud of his product as it is stamped with his name in five places. "Otto Evers-maker—Fredericksburg, Tex." Early 1900s. It is a fine, old, A-fork Texas cowboy saddle. Collection: Joe Gish.

A beautiful, early 1900s California saddle made by Main and Winchester of San Francisco, California and marked on the back of the seat. Collection: Joe Gish.

This saddle was made for Joseph C. Miller, one of three brothers who were partners in the 101 Ranch Wild West show. It was made in 1913 at a reported cost of $5,800. The nickle silver horn is capped with a gold and silver crown containing 24 rubies, 16 sapphires and 9 diamonds, plus one large diamond in the middle. The 5½'' cantle has a silver filigreed plate set with diamonds, rubies and sapphires, spelling 101 ranch. A back panel on the cantle spells Joseph C. Miller's. Billed as the "finest saddle in the world" it was a featured attraction in the show. With a total of 293 stones mounted in nearly 18 pounds of silver and gold, such a claim was not an exaggeration. Collection: Texas Ranger Museum, Waco, Texas.

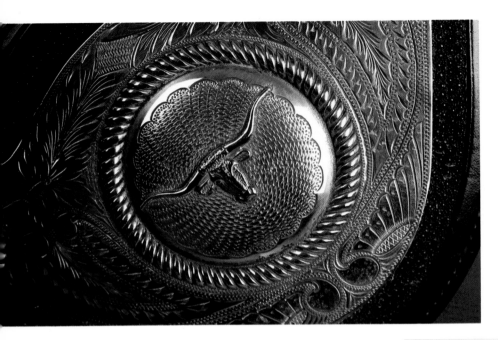

Silver mounted parade saddle with a breast collar, corona, *tapaderos* and bridle, circa 1930, made by Edward H. Bohlin. This distinctive parade outfit with high cantel and swell fork construction was called the "San Fernando" model by Bohlin. Collection: George Pitman.

Fancy dress saddle by Keyston, San Francisco, California. circa 1930s. This saddle is mounted in silver and finely engraved. Keyston was one of the finest saddle makers as evidenced by this example. Collection: Michael Friedman.

A fine California parade saddle, made in 1930 by Bryden Brothers of Los Angeles, California. Especially made for Teddy Arrigone, who rode with Tom Mix and Leo Carrillo. Collection: George Pitman.

Fine silver mounted saddle with silver trim and inlaid silver horn by G.S. Garcia of Elko, Nevada, circa 1924. The stirrups are steel with engraved silver overlay of an eagle and shield, and stars and stripes. Collection: C.W. Lyle, Jr.

Miniatures

A beautiful miniature, hand-carved A-fork saddle marked "F. Ronstadt Co., Makers, Tucson, Az.," circa 1920. The saddle is complete with *tapaderos* and woven horsehair cinch, 17" long and 26" high. It was used in a Wild West show for a monkey who rode a goat. (Note the goat carved on the jockeys.) Collection: Joe Gish.

Rare, miniature "Texas Hope" style saddle with a 9"-wide and 6"-long skirt and 2½" wide horn, circa 1870s. The portions of the saddle not covered by leather are covered with rawhide. This saddle vividly displays the development from the Mexican style to the Old Texas trail driver's style. Collection: Jim Holley.

Early salesman's sample saddle. Collection: Jim Holley.

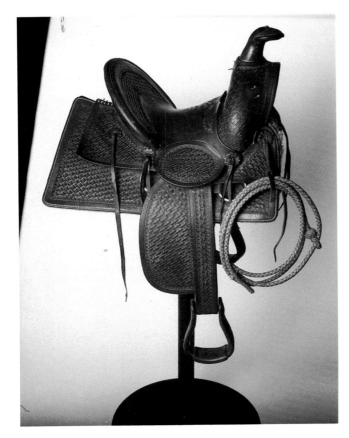

Saddlemaker S.D. Myres began his career in Sweetwater, Texas and moved his growing business to El Paso in 1920. This salesman's sample saddle is marked "S.D. Myres, Sweetwater, Texas" and is a fine example of his early work in Sweetwater. Collection: C.W. Lyle, Jr.

Fine example of a salesman's sample saddle, circa 1915. Salesmen's samples are half the size of a full saddle. Note the finely detailed basket-weave design and the nickel horn. Collection: Jim Holley.

A salesman's sample saddle made by W.H. Smith of Oklahoma City, Oklahoma, circa 1930s. Collection: C.W. Lyle, Jr.

A fine and rare salesman's sample of a Texas marked half seat saddle. Signed: G.&A. Hoefner, Flatonia Texas. 7'' seat and 13'' skirts. Circa 1875. Apple horn and Angora Anqueros. Collection: Dave VanMeter.

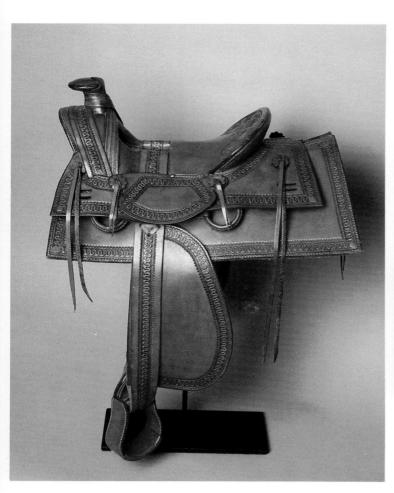

Salesman's sample of an early, tooled, half seat saddle with Sam Stagg rigging. While this saddle depicts a circa 1880 trail saddle, it was actually made in the 1960s. Collection: Michael Friedman.

Salesman sample of a saddle tree, sewn leather over wood. Collection: Michael Friedman.

Tooled minature saddle, circa pre-1920s, which was purchased from a family in Montana whose grandfather owned the saddle and worked for Main & Winchester in San Francisco. Even though the saddle is unmarked, it probably was made in the Main & Winchester shop. Collection: Jim Holley.

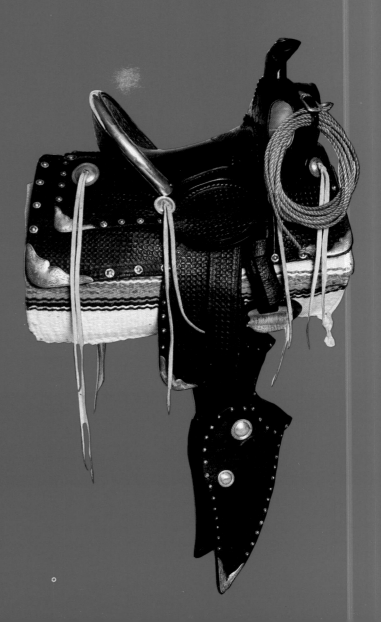

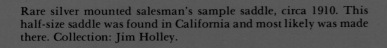

Rare silver mounted salesman's sample saddle, circa 1910. This half-size saddle was found in California and most likely was made there. Collection: Jim Holley.

Late 19th century folk painting of Vaqueros at a picnic. Their costumes and acoutrements show the fashion of the period. Collection: Michael Friedman.

Vaquero

This saddle belonged to this collector's great-grandfather, a Mexican Colonel who fought the French in 1864. Collection: Enrique Guerra.

Mexican saddle, circa 1870, with a heavy horn, silver cantel, and some embroidery trim. A machete is mounted at the side. This is not a working saddle, but not a sunday-best either. Collection: Enrique Guerra.

A very early Mexican saddle, circa 1850s to 1860s, with a very high and large horn, silver cantel and stirrups. The skirts are most unusual with rawhide carved roses and leaf stems. Note the angora saddle bags. Collection: Enrique Guerra.

A Mexican saddle made in Puebla Mexico at the turn of the century. The leather is beautifully tooled and trimmed with silver and a Mexican eagle horn, circa 1890s to 1900. This particular saddle was made especially for William Randolph Hearst's father. Collection: Enrique Guerra.

A late Mexican saddle with mounted silver, silver thread embroidery, and unsually fine silver work on the horn, cantel and stirrups. This saddle was presented to the President of Mexico, Don Venutiano Carranza in 1914. Collection: Enrique Guerra.

Mexican silver mounted saddle with cactus fiber embroidery, circa 1880-1890, with a Liberty cap emblem on the horn. Collection: Enrique Guerra.

In the early days in Texas, in the sixties, when they gathered their cattle, they used to pack what they needed on a horse and go out for weeks, on a cow-hunt, they called it then. That was before the name roundup was invented, and before they had anything so civilized as mess wagons. And as I say, that is the way those first trail hands were raised.

We Pointed Them North

Saddlebags

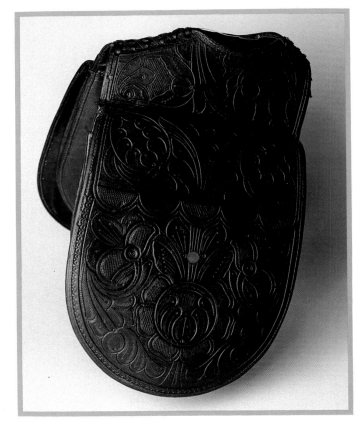

Beautifully carved California pommel saddle bags with straps inside to hold a revolver. An early style, circa 1880 to 1890, it is in nice condition for its age. Collection: Joe Gish.

Finely carved unmarked saddle bags, circa 1930s. Maker: N. Porter. Collection: High Noon.

Early California pommel bags with built-in holster on one side. Circa 1890. Maker: Main and Winchester. Collection: Jerard Paul Jordan.

Possibly a salesman's sample, these small saddlebags were made by C.P. Shipley of Kansas City Missouri. Shipley was in business from 1885-1967. Collection: Vic Williams.

Interesting pair of saddle pockets with bear fur on the flaps. The under flaps are marked: "Lohlein & Sigwait, Laramie, Wyo." This maker, in business between 1895 and 1906, was sometimes known as The Laramie Saddle Co. Collection: Joe Gish.

Nice old pair of cowboy saddle bags marked on both sides, "F.A. Meanea, Cheyenne, Wyo.," circa early-1900s. Collection: Joe Gish.

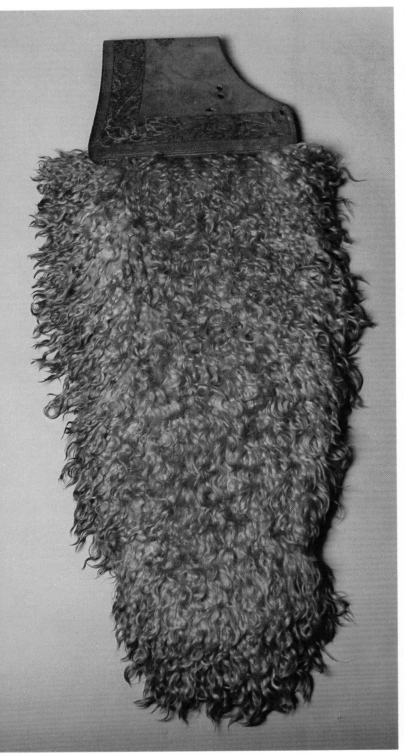

Orange Angora Serapes with border tooling, circa 1920s to 1930s. Billings, Montana. Collection: Jerard Paul Jordan.

Fine pair of white angora saddle pockets, circa 1920, made by R.T. Frazier of Pueblo Colorado. Collection: Jerard Paul Jordan.

Rope

Four-strand reata with extra fine honda which looks like a snake's head. Collection: Dave Van Meter.

Braided leather horse hobbles. Collection: C.W. Lyle, Jr.

A well made eight strand braided leather quirt from the early 1900's. Collection: Vic Williams.

Ortega

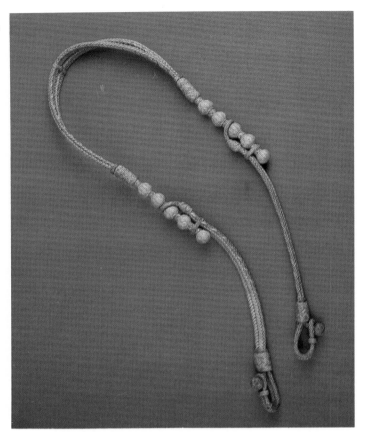

Rawhide reins made by Luis Ortega in the Santa Inez style from the early 1940s. The reins, are eight strands of spotted skin rawhide and the romel is 16 strands spotted skin rawhide. Made for Ken Fratis at the Lompoc grammar school. The reins are signed by the maker and marked "Ken Fratis" on the popper. Collection: High Noon.

A rawhide headstall made for Ken Fratis, a schoolmate of Ortegas, at the Lompoc grammar school, by Luis Ortega, circa early 1940s. Double-three all natural red durham rawhide strands are laced together. Collection: High Noon.

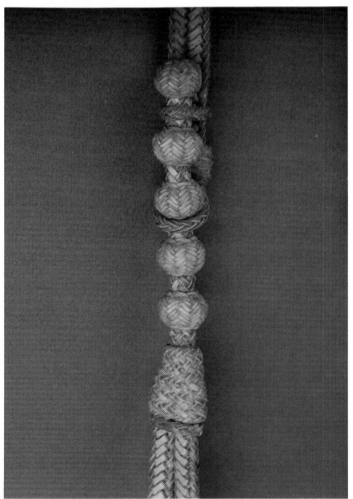

A fine rawhide Reata made for Lloyd B. Taggart of Las Vegas, N.M. by Luis Ortega, circa 1970s, from twelve strands of natural rawhide with red rawhide trim on honda. It is signed "LBT" and "LBO" on the honda. Collection: High Noon.

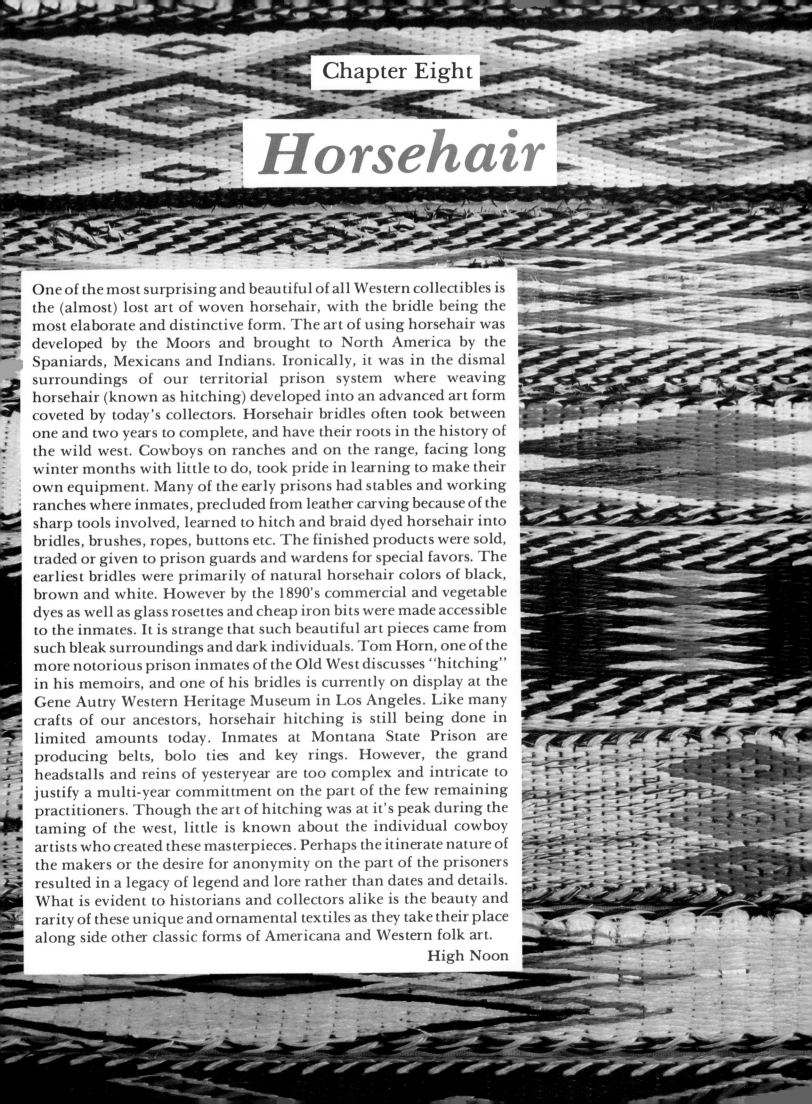

Chapter Eight

Horsehair

One of the most surprising and beautiful of all Western collectibles is the (almost) lost art of woven horsehair, with the bridle being the most elaborate and distinctive form. The art of using horsehair was developed by the Moors and brought to North America by the Spaniards, Mexicans and Indians. Ironically, it was in the dismal surroundings of our territorial prison system where weaving horsehair (known as hitching) developed into an advanced art form coveted by today's collectors. Horsehair bridles often took between one and two years to complete, and have their roots in the history of the wild west. Cowboys on ranches and on the range, facing long winter months with little to do, took pride in learning to make their own equipment. Many of the early prisons had stables and working ranches where inmates, precluded from leather carving because of the sharp tools involved, learned to hitch and braid dyed horsehair into bridles, brushes, ropes, buttons etc. The finished products were sold, traded or given to prison guards and wardens for special favors. The earliest bridles were primarily of natural horsehair colors of black, brown and white. However by the 1890's commercial and vegetable dyes as well as glass rosettes and cheap iron bits were made accessible to the inmates. It is strange that such beautiful art pieces came from such bleak surroundings and dark individuals. Tom Horn, one of the more notorious prison inmates of the Old West discusses "hitching" in his memoirs, and one of his bridles is currently on display at the Gene Autry Western Heritage Museum in Los Angeles. Like many crafts of our ancestors, horsehair hitching is still being done in limited amounts today. Inmates at Montana State Prison are producing belts, bolo ties and key rings. However, the grand headstalls and reins of yesteryear are too complex and intricate to justify a multi-year committment on the part of the few remaining practitioners. Though the art of hitching was at it's peak during the taming of the west, little is known about the individual cowboy artists who created these masterpieces. Perhaps the itinerate nature of the makers or the desire for anonymity on the part of the prisoners resulted in a legacy of legend and lore rather than dates and details. What is evident to historians and collectors alike is the beauty and rarity of these unique and ornamental textiles as they take their place along side other classic forms of Americana and Western folk art.

High Noon

Previous page:
Collection of fine horsehair belts. Collection: High Noon.

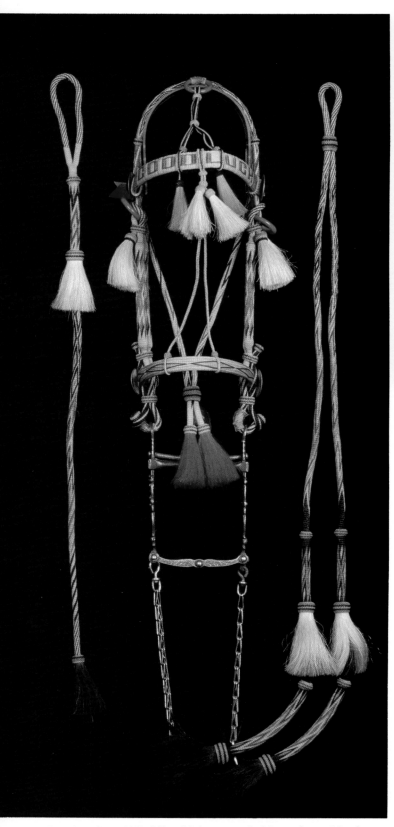

Deerlodge hitched horsehair brush with American flag design, circa 1920s to 1930s. Though bridles and belts were the most popular of the prison horsehair items, purses, watch fobs, gavels, hatbands, buttons, ropes, quirts and even suspenders also were made. Collection: High Noon.

The "Good Luck" bridle which was probably made at a Northwest prison, circa 1900 to 1910, including a headstall, reins and romal. Slogans and dates were occasionally woven into the brow- and nose-bands. Collection: High Noon.

Note the excellent detail work and typical Southwestern colors on a Yuma bridle from the 1900s. Also the intricate checkerboard pattern. Collection: High Noon.

A colorful, hitched horsehair headstall with the typical Deerlodge colors of natural (light) background and bold, geometric colored patterns. These colors are strong and show no evidence of fading. However, most horsehair bridles were made with light-sensitive aniline dyes that faded after being exposed to direct, indirect or artificial light. Collection: High Noon.

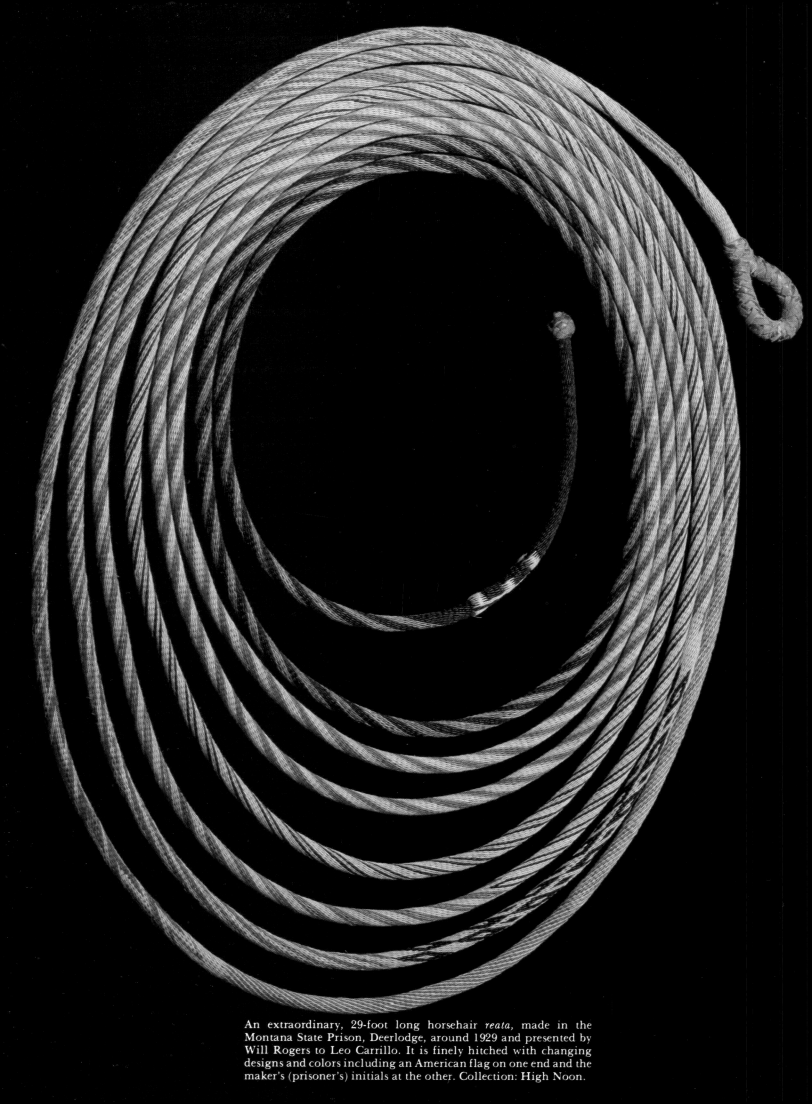

An extraordinary, 29-foot long horsehair *reata*, made in the
Montana State Prison, Deerlodge, around 1929 and presented by
Will Rogers to Leo Carrillo. It is finely hitched with changing
designs and colors including an American flag on one end and the
maker's (prisoner's) initials at the other. Collection: High Noon.

A stunning double-sided, hitched horsehair hatband whose origin and maker are unknown but was probably made in the 1930s. Some old horsehair hatbands may have been belts that have been cut down. Collection: High Noon.

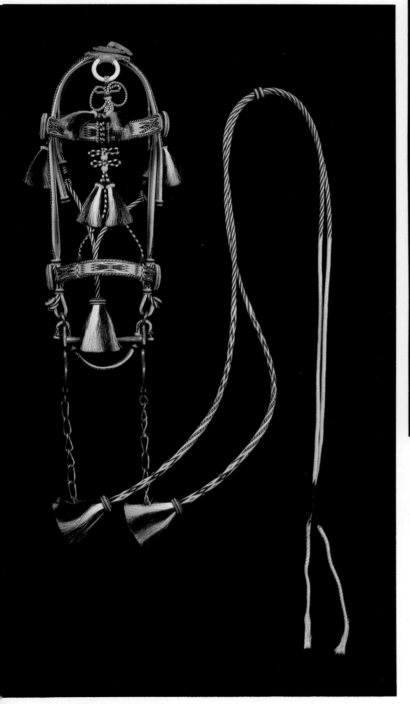

Made at the Arizona Territoral Prison at Yuma, this hitched and wrapped horsehair bridle, pre-1910, has a characteristic flat browband that is both wrapped and hitched with braided and large hitched conchos (not comercially made glass rosettes like Deerlodge and Walla Walla). The colors are typically southwestern: red, orange, yellow, black and maroon. Collection: High Noon.

Natural-colored horsehair bridle, probably made at Deerlodge judging from the finish of the reins. Commercially made glass rosettes are trimmed in horsehair. The bit is typical, inexpensive, and commercially-made, circa 1910. Collection: High Noon.

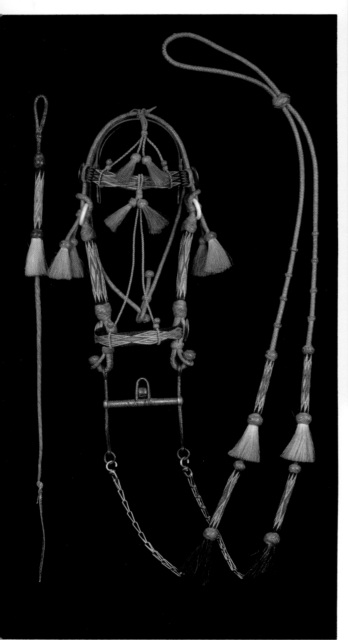

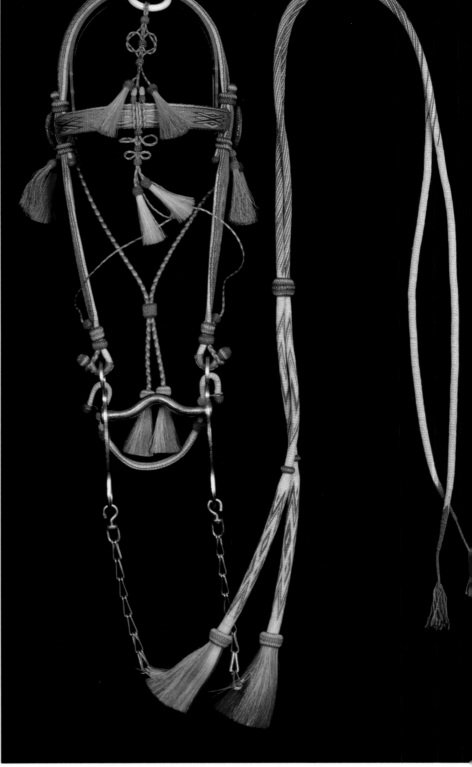

An unusual bright pink horsehair bridle from the Northwest, circa 1910. Collection: High Noon.

A combination braided kangaroo and hitched horsehair headstall, reins, and romal. Probably made in Rallens Prison, Wyoming in the 1920s. Collection: High Noon.

Chapter Nine

Bits

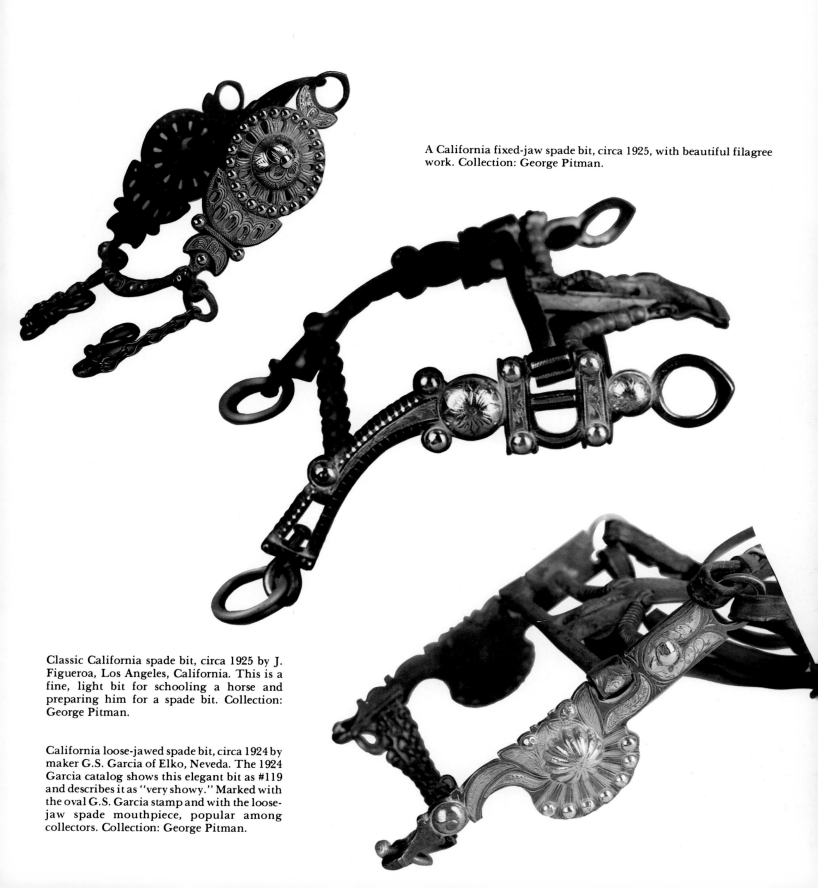

A California fixed-jaw spade bit, circa 1925, with beautiful filagree work. Collection: George Pitman.

Classic California spade bit, circa 1925 by J. Figueroa, Los Angeles, California. This is a fine, light bit for schooling a horse and preparing him for a spade bit. Collection: George Pitman.

California loose-jawed spade bit, circa 1924 by maker G.S. Garcia of Elko, Neveda. The 1924 Garcia catalog shows this elegant bit as #119 and describes it as "very showy." Marked with the oval G.S. Garcia stamp and with the loose-jaw spade mouthpiece, popular among collectors. Collection: George Pitman.

A California silver gal-leg bit, circa 1920s and marked "G.C." on the inside. Collection: C.W. Lyle, Jr.

A fancy crescent half-breed California bit, circa 1911, made by G.S. Garcia of Elko, Nevada. A classic Garcia bit, it is shown as bit #60 in his 1911 catalog. Collection: George Pitman.

A silver engraved California roller bit. Collection: C.W. Lyle, Jr.

Early California loose-jawed spade bit, circa 1890, by Marduno, an early California maker. Collection: George Pitman.

Left: A California silver, half-breed roller bit with an interesting heart motif, circa 1920s characteristic Mike Morales Jello mold concho. Collection: C.W. Lyle, Jr.

Right: Unmarked Mike Morales style silver inlaid Santa Barbara spade bit. Collection: C.W. Lyle, Jr.

California half breed bit, circa 1925, with deep engraving and fine filagree work. Collection: George Pitman.

They used to have some terrible storms on the North and South Platte. The year before this, in '82, I was in one that killed fourteen head of cattle and six or seven horses and two men, on the different herds. One man was so scared he threw his six-shooter away for fear it would draw the lightening; and I remember old Matt Winter, with the rain apouring down and the lightning flashing, taking off his hat and yelling at God Almighty: "All right, you old bald-headed son of a bitch up there, if you want to kill me, come on do it!" It scared the daylights out of the rest of us.

We Pointed Them North

A California silver overlay engraved bit by G.S. Garcia of Elko, Nevada. Collection: Roger Baker.

California fixed-jaw spade bit, circa 1920. Collection: George Pitman.

A California silver overlay engraved bit by G.S. Garcia of Elko, Nevada. Collection: Roger Baker.

A California silver overlay bit with a folksy-looking eagle, circa 1920s. Collection: Roger Baker.

A silver spade bit with an engraved California eagle, circa 1925. Collection: George Pitman.

Bit with medallion shank and eagle lip bar. Circa 1925. Maker: Ralph W. Graham, Joseph, Oregon. Few examples of Graham's work are known. Collection: George Pitman.

California spade bit with 10k gold overlayed spots and initials, circa 1939 made by G.S. Garcia after he moved to Salinas, California. This fine bit was previously owned by prominent California rancher Harry West. Collection: George Pitman.

California loose-jawed spade bit with 10k gold overlay, circa 1930, made by R. Gutierrez for Gunner Thornberg, a noted horseman of the 1920s and 1930's. Collection: George Pitman.

An early silver California bit, circa 1935, made by Ed Field of Santa Barbara, California. Collection: Carole S. Statler.

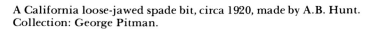

A California loose-jawed spade bit, circa 1920, made by A.B. Hunt. Collection: George Pitman.

A California spade bit, circa 1920. Note the owl face depicted on the top of the shank. Collection: George Pitman.

A silver mounted, six-gun bit engraved "New Mexico" on one cheek and "Arizona" on the other which was made to celebrate the admission of Arizona and New Mexico into the union. Collection: High Noon.

A nicely engraved California silver overlay bit, circa 1920, by R. Filo Gutierrez of San Francisco, California. The high quality of this bit is typical of Gutierrez's work. Collection: Carole S. Statler.

Made in the Colorado State Prison, this bit was signed only by the prisioner's number #4307. The inmate was convicted murderer John Cox who died while serving a life term at the Cañon City Prison in 1940. Silver engraved overlay and abalone grips add greatly to the beauty of this piece, circa turn of the century. Collection: Michael Friedman.

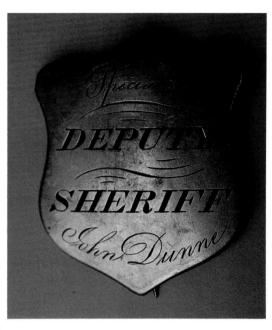

Nickel plated Special Deputy Sheriff badge in the shape of a shield. It is unusual for a Special Deputy Sheriff badge to be custom engraved and to include the officer's name. Collection: Michael Friedman.

A nickel plated, brass Deputy Sheriff badge, with safety pin catch and enamel lettering. Made by Ed Jones and Company, Oakland, California. Circa 1890-1930. Collection: Vic Williams.

Ed Jones and Company was one of the most prominent badge makers of the West. This reverse painted glass sign is a "one of a kind" which hung on the front door of their Oakland office, circa 1890s. Collection: Roger Baker.

Classic ball tipped star badge. This is a stock badge used throughout the west in the old days. Collection: Michael Friedman.

Collection: Michael Friedman.

Chapter Ten

Badges

Hand engraved, coin silver hat badge, pre-1900, with an early J-pin and steel catch. Collection: Vic Williams.

Collecting badges of the Old West can be a bit tricky. To begin with, the early classic badges are rare, but relatively easy to reproduce. Their rarity makes them expensive and, as with other antiques which are valuable and reproducible, badges have suffered greatly in recent years from a proliferation of reproductions. It is important to distinguish here between fakes and reproductions.

The major contemporary manufacturer produces and markets badges on a normal wholesale/retail basis with no claim of their being from the early period. Unfortunately, these badges are virtually indistinguishable from the old versions, (at least to the average person or collector). There is no mark which would indicate that these badges are new and often they end up being sold as old. And badges made about 20 years ago are even harder to distinguish. This is not to say that genuine badges of the early period are not available or identifiable; good dealers of Western antiques will know the difference and be willing to advise the collector and guarantee authenticity.

With that being said, badges are among the most interesting and varied of Western items. They hold a special place in the legend of the Old West since they represent the "good guy", the strong, fearless lawman who kept the peace and protected the citizenry.

There are two major types of old badges: the stock badge, and the custom badge. Stock badges are most commonly encountered since they were produced in relatively large numbers and could be used by any law enforcement department anywhere in the country. Since they were generic in nature, they often had a title that could easily be assigned from one person to another. For example, most basic police, constable, or deputy badges are stock. Custom badges, on the other hand, were ordered for a specific lawman such as a marshal, a sheriff or a ranger. These badges were not stamped out like the stock badges but rather were individually made and the more elaborate ones contain gold or silver, precious stones, enameling or fine engraving. Obviously the more elaborate, the more valuable, especially if the officer was a known person or if the location was a historic Western town.

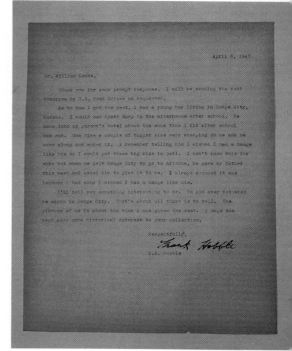

This wool vest belonged to the famous lawman Wyatt Earp. It is accompanied by a letter explaining how Earp had given it to a young boy. Collection: Lang Spraggins.

Extraordinary gold Chief of Police badge with ruby eyes in the eagle and a total of eleven rubies. It is exceptionally large, circa 1915, Los Angeles, California. An inscription is on the reverse. Collection: C.W. Lyle, Jr.

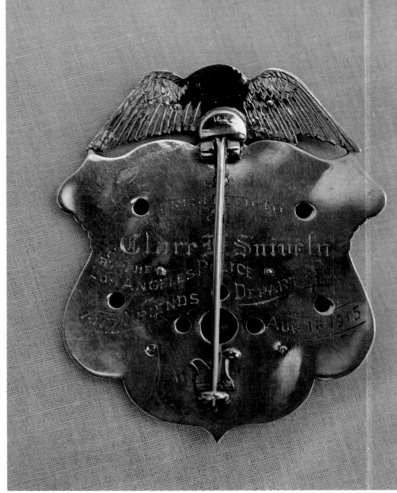

And I was really dangerous. A kid is more dangerous than a man because he's so sensitive about his personal courage. He's just itching to shoot somebody in order to prove himself. I did shoot a man once. I was only sixteen, and drunk. A bunch of us left town on a dead run, shooting at the gas lamps. I was in the lead and the town marshal was right in front of me with his gun in his hand calling, "Halt! Halt! Throw 'em up!" And I throwed 'em up all right, right in his face. I always had that idea in my head—"Shoot your way out." I did not go to town for a long time afterwards, but he never knew who shot him, because it was dark enough so he could not see.

We Pointed Them North

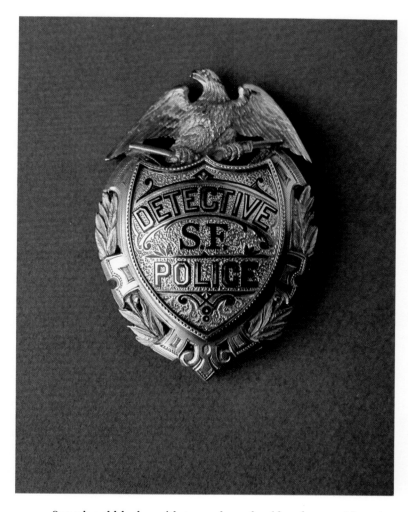

Superb gold badge with two colors of gold and enamel lettering, circa 1880, made by D.W. Laird of San Francisco, California. It belonged to Edward "Ned" Byran, who was a noted San Francisco police detective in the years from 1876 to 1908. Custom badges of this quality from the Old West are rare. Collection: J. Boessenecker.

Fine City Marshal badge. Desirable form, from the turn of the century. Collection: Michael Friedman.

Gold badge from Hidalgo County, Texas near the Mexican border. This is a handsome, custom-made badge. Collection: Enrique Guerra.

"Tin" badges representative of those worn by lawmen of the Old West. This group of sheriff, deputy sheriff and constable badges are from New Mexico, California, Washington, Utah, Kansas, Nevada, Montana, and Arizona. They are the classic Old Western style. Collection: Joe Gish.

Group of old lawmen's "stock" badges with no state, city, or county name on them. They were used by any agency anywhere. Many were sold direct to law offices by "drummers," traveling salesmen. Most are made from brass with nickel plating; some are made from German silver and unplated. They are desirable among Western collectors. Collection: Joe Gish.

Reverse-painted glass sheriff's sign, circa 1915 to 1925. Collection:
C.W. Lyle, Jr.

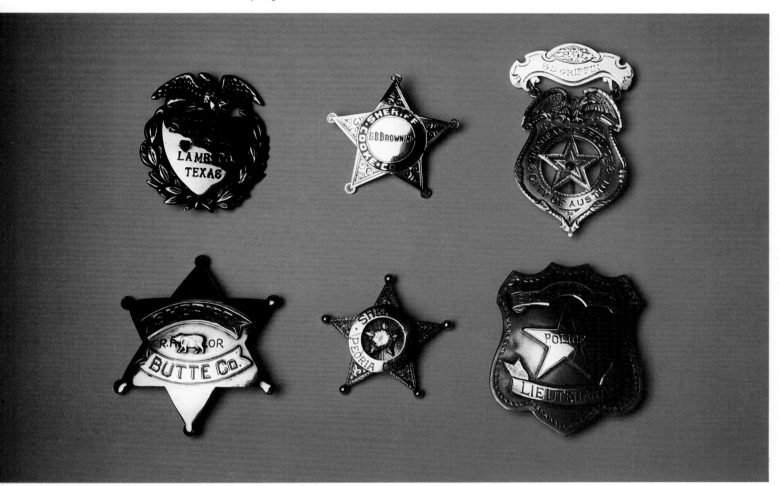

Beautiful group of badges. The Lamb Co. badge is brass, the Salt
Lake badge is silver and gold, and all others are solid gold. Gold
badges were always made for a special order and were expensive and
much rarer than brass or nickel. Collection: C.W. Lyle, Jr.

Left, Early Indian police badge. Right, United States Marshal cut-out star badge. Collection: C. W. Lyle, Jr.

Early law enforcement badges. Left, Deputy Sheriff, Galveston. Center, Deputy Marshal. Right, Ft. Worth Police No. 1, circa early 1900s. Collection: C. W. Lyle, Jr.

This nickel plated brass, six-point star stock badge was typical of the type used by lawmen throughout the country at the turn of the century. Collection: Michael Friedman.

Early Dallas County, Texas badge with a rare Texas longhorn motif, circa 1910. Collection: C. W. Lyle, Jr.

Early twentieth century Texas Deputy Sheriff badge with the officer's name at the top. Collection: Michael Friedman.

Early Indian police badge. Collection: C. W. Lyle, Jr.

Stock badge with custom initials from a Utah lawman. Circa turn of the century. Collection: Vic Williams.

Deputy City Marshal's badge, early 1900s, stamped nickel with enamel lettering and safety pin catch. Collection: Vic Williams.

Special Police badge, pre-1900, heavy German silver, enameled with a T-pin clasp. Collection: Vic Williams.

Old Texas lawman's badge. Collection: Enrique Guerra.

Very large Constable star badge, circa 1880 to 1890. Collection: C.W. Lyle, Jr.

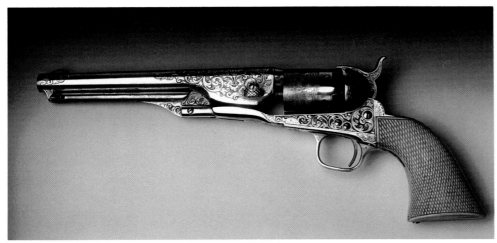

Colt model 1861 revolver with Nimschke engraving and checkered ivory grips in excellent condition. Collection: C.W. Lyle, Jr.

Rare factory-engraved Bisley with carved steer head and ivory grips. Collection: Enrique Guerra.

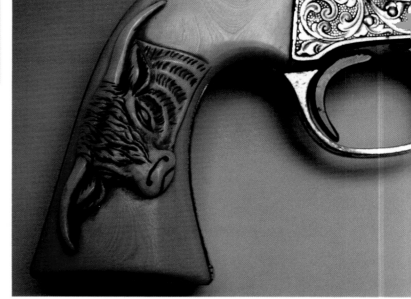

Down in Texas in the early days every man had to have his six shooter always ready, every house kept a shotgun loaded with buckshot, because they were always looking for a raid by Mexicans or Comanche Indians.

We Pointed Them North

Chapter Eleven

Guns

There is perhaps no greater icon of the Old West than the famed Colt Peacemaker or Single Action Army gun. Introduced in 1873, Samuel Colt designed a revolver which was to become the West's most desired, best remembered and most collected gun. Produced in a number of different calibers and offered by the factory in various finishes, barrel lengths and grips, the Colt SAA's greatest advantages over earlier models were that it took center-fire cartridges, was made of heavier metal, carried more powder and was less likely to misfire. They were strong and reliable and had an effective range of about 100 yards with an overall range of some 400 yards. Other popular frontier revolvers included the 1.) Smith and Wesson Russian, 2.) Smith and Wesson Schofield [used by Wells Fargo & Co. and by Jesse James], 3.) Remington Army .44 [designed to compete albeit unsuccessfully with the colt S.A.A.], 4.) Merwin & Hulbert Army, and, 5.) Colt Frontier double action .45 model.

During the open range or early period of the cowboy [1840-1870] percussion revolvers were used, the most popular of which was the Colt 1851 Navy. Because these percussion revolvers were slow to reload, many cowboys took to carrying two guns. In the 1870s, self-contained metallic cartridges were introduced to eliminate the need to carry two guns. In 1873, Colt introduced the Single Action with the entire initial production purchased by the U.S. Army. It wasn't until 1875 that this gun became available to the civilian market and from that time on it became known as the cowboy sixgun.

It is fair to say that until the revolver, the white man was no match for the Indian in the Old West. The indian knew that after one shot the white man had to reload. All he needed to do was wait until that one shot was fired before he unleashed a dozen or so arrows. The first recorded use of the revolver took place at Enchanted Rock, Texas in 1841. Jack Hayes found himself trapped by a band of Apaches who assumed that after the first shot, they would have time to attack. They hadn't figured on the five-shot Colt Patterson which Hayes possessed and which turned the balance of power of that and future confrontations distinctly in the white man's favor.

Colonel Colt had introduced the Patterson model (so named because the factory was located in Patterson, N.J.) in 1836. The Patterson proved to be so unpopular and expensive that Colt went bankrupt in 1842. In 1845 when Texas became a state, Captain Sam Walker approached Samuel Colt with an idea for a revolver to be used by the Texas Rangers to defend Texas against a myriad of adversaries including outlaws, Indians, rustlers, and Mexican *banditos.* That collaboration produced a revolver that propelled the Colt operation into one of the most important and successful ventures in American history. Mass production in America was born in the Colt factory in Hartford, Connecticut and with it, Col. Colt became America's first industrial tycoon. Colt sealed his success with the outbreak of the Civil War, selling arms to both sides, and ultimately contributing to there being 4 million guns in private hands at the end of the war.

It was common for a man to carry a derringer, (also known as a "tuckaway" or "hide-out" gun). Named after Henry Deringer, Jr. (and later misspelled "derringer") this became the generic name for all small pocket pistols. Derringers were also the gun of choice among women since they could be secreted in a garter, a halter or handbag. The most popular derringer was the .41 caliber, Remington 2-shot, "over and under" of which more than 150,000 were produced. Whether carried by regular citizens as a means of protection, as a back-up gun by lawmen and outlaws, or as a hide-out gun by gamblers and hucksters, these little beauties played an important role in the Old West.

The Colt S.A.A. "Judge Colt and his jury of Six". God created man, but Col. Colt made them equal.

Two rare, Colt 3rd model Dragoons, factory engraved with Mexican eagle carved grips. Only six are known to exist like this which left the factory gold and silver plated. Collection: Enrique Guerra.

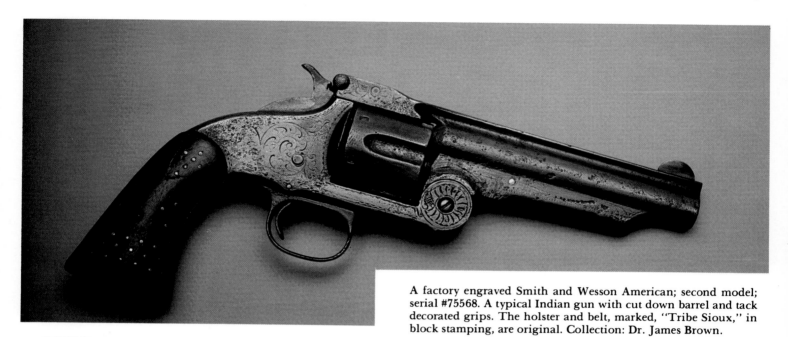

A factory engraved Smith and Wesson American; second model; serial #75568. A typical Indian gun with cut down barrel and tack decorated grips. The holster and belt, marked, "Tribe Sioux," in block stamping, are original. Collection: Dr. James Brown.

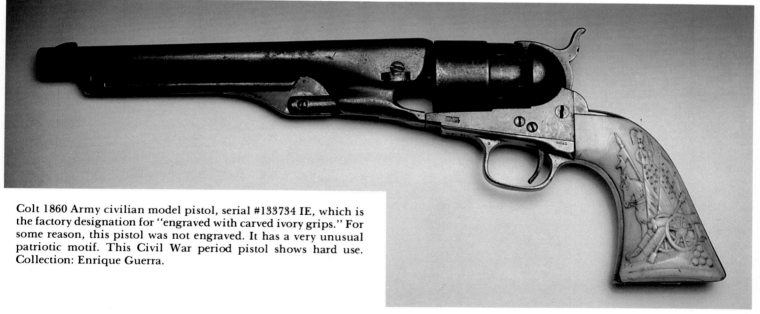

Colt 1860 Army civilian model pistol, serial #133734 IE, which is the factory designation for "engraved with carved ivory grips." For some reason, this pistol was not engraved. It has a very unusual patriotic motif. This Civil War period pistol shows hard use. Collection: Enrique Guerra.

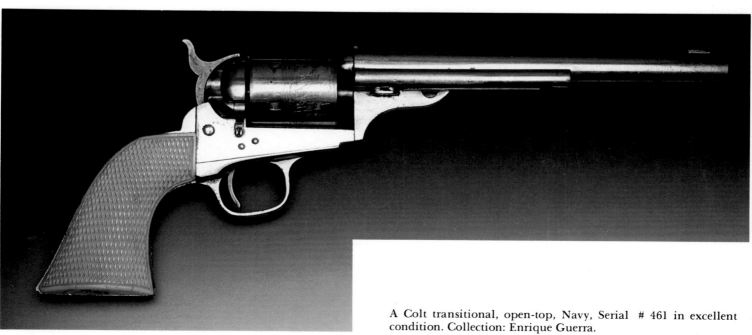

A Colt transitional, open-top, Navy, Serial # 461 in excellent condition. Collection: Enrique Guerra.

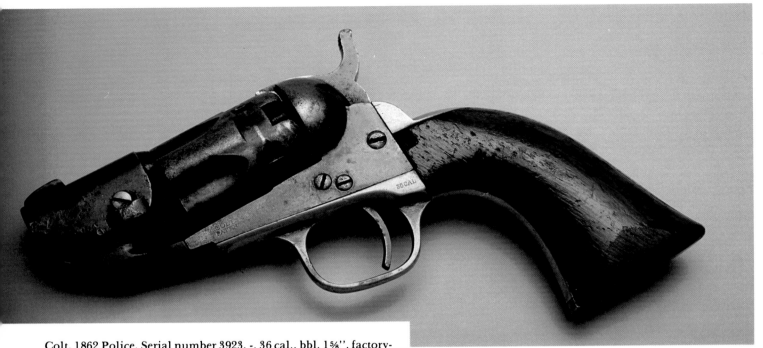

Colt, 1862 Police, Serial number 3923, -. 36 cal., bbl. 1⅝'', factory-altered to a snub-nose type which was done only on special order. These were made during the Civil War period and were used by spies, Pinkertons and gamblers. The notches on the inside of the grips are very old and interesting, but their reason is unknown. Collection: Dr. James Brown.

Smith & Wesson (model No: 3) second model single action revolver, circa 1872 to 1874, .44 cal. with 8'' barrel. Collection: Vic Williams.

A Colt, 3rd model Dragoon, Serial #19277, .44 cal., 8'' barrel, with walnut stocks and silver inlays. In serial range 18,000 and 19,000, only a few pistols were manufactured with 8'' barrels so today they are scarce. Collection: Enrique Guerra.

3rd model Dragoon with shoulder stock. Collection: Dr. James Brown.

Colt 1862 Police pistol, serial #29830 with fine carved ivory grips depicting an American eagle on top of the word "Liberty." Collection: Enrique Guerra.

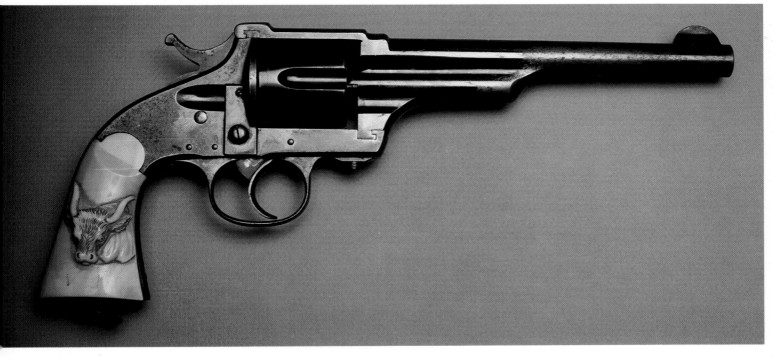

Merwin and Hulbert, .44 cal. revolvers were popular in the Old West. Note the unusual steer's head carved on the ivory grips of this one, serial # 18213. Collection: Enrique Guerra.

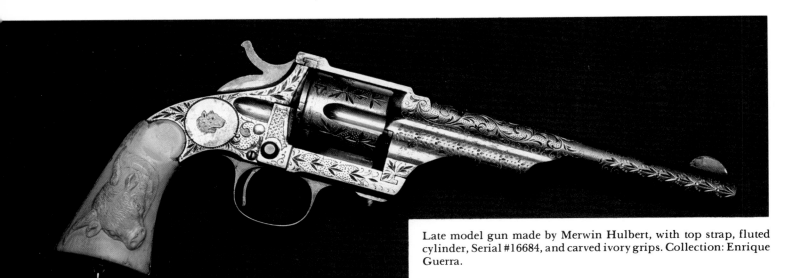

Late model gun made by Merwin Hulbert, with top strap, fluted cylinder, Serial #16684, and carved ivory grips. Collection: Enrique Guerra.

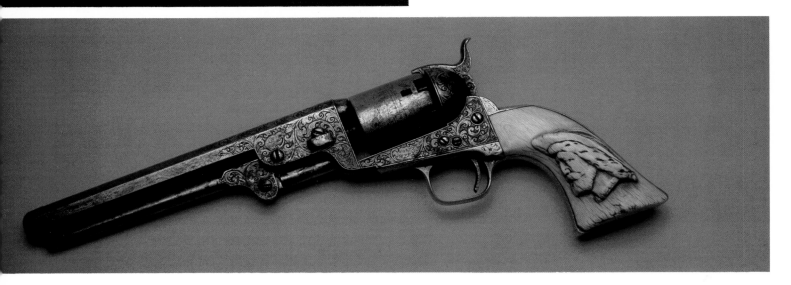

Circa 1851, Navy colt, serial 91143, factory engraved and with what appears to be factory ivory grips. The carved ivory face is usually referred to as a "Cavalier," although some call it a "Mountain Man" Collection: Dr. James Brown.

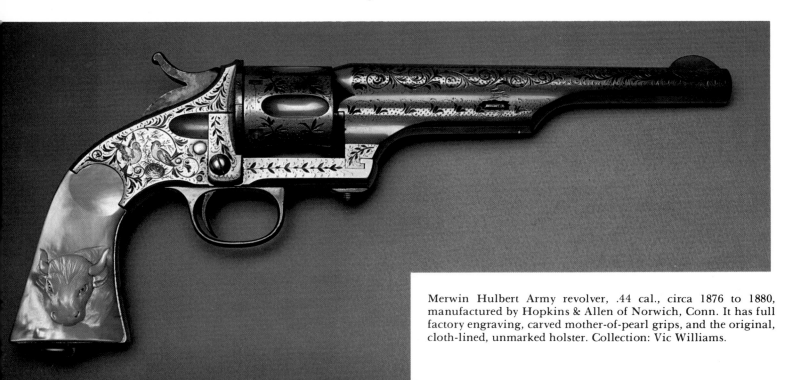

Merwin Hulbert Army revolver, .44 cal., circa 1876 to 1880, manufactured by Hopkins & Allen of Norwich, Conn. It has full factory engraving, carved mother-of-pearl grips, and the original, cloth-lined, unmarked holster. Collection: Vic Williams.

But I wouldn't give mine up. A six-shooter's an awful lot of company. Suppose you break your leg, you can signal. If you're caught afoot, you can shoot a jack rabbit. If you're held up, you can defend yourself.

We Pointed Them North

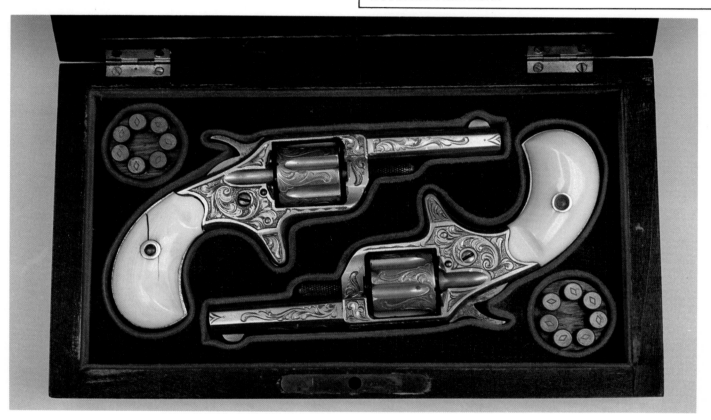

Cased Colt .22 revolvers with ivory grips and engraved gold cylinders made by the Colt Mfg. Co. of Hartford, Connecticut, Patented Sept. 15, 1874. Collection: C.W. Lyle, Jr.

An engraved, 4¾'' bbl., black powder colt S.A.A. shipped to Austin, Texas. The carved pearl steerhead grips feature a silver Texas star inset. Possibly a lawman's gun. Collection: Enrique Guerra.

Rare Remington double derringer .41 cal. rim fire with rosewood grips, serial # 20, and the earliest markings, by E. Remington & Sons of Elion, New York, circa 1866. Collection: Vic Williams.

Remington pearl gripped Over and Under derringer along with a superb gold badge. Circa 1880. Badge maker: D.W. Laird, San Francisco, California. This pair belong to Edward "Ned" Byran, who was a noted S.F. police detective in the years 1876-1908. Two colors of gold and enamel lettering. Custom badges of this quality from the old west are rare. Collection: J. Boessenecker.

Remington double derringer .41 cal. Rim-Fire 1st model, with ivory grips, rare, circa late-1860s. Collection: Vic Williams.

Engraved, .45 automatic pistol, serial #26244, which was engraved by Ken Hunt, showing a Mexican cowboy roping a horse. The holster is decorated in silver repossee, ivory grips. Collection: Enrique Guerra.

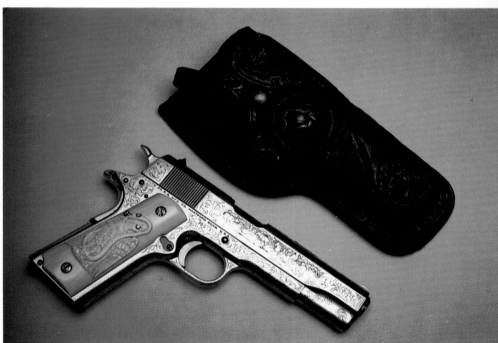

One of two consectutively numbered .45 automatics. This one engraved by Frank Hendricks depicting Mexicans stealing cattle in Texas, branding them and going through cut barbed wire fences. It has the original factory ivory grips, a Mexican eagle and snake with diamond eyes and a holster made in Mexico with three-dimensional embroidered rows of gold and silver thread, Serial Num: 70G14538. Collection: Enrique Guerra.

A Colt lightning, serial #18419, with factory engraving and carved pearl grips depicting grapes, possibly custom made for a California vintner. Collection: Enrique Guerra.

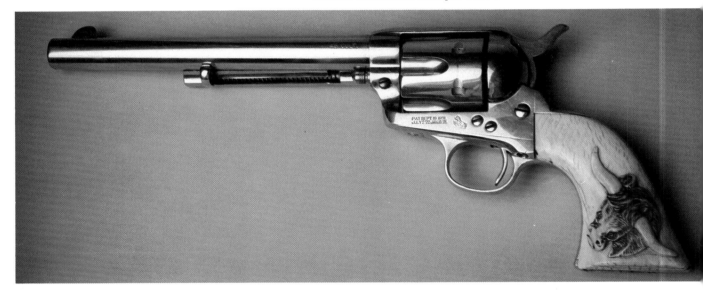

Colt S.A.A. with 7½'' barrel, and carved ivory grips. Factory nickel re-finished. Collection: C.W. Lyle, Jr.

Moore 1st model .41 cal., engraved and gold and silver plated, in excellent condition. Collection: C.W. Lyle, Jr.

Factory engraved Remington Elliot derringer, .22 cal. rim fire, 5 shots, circa 1863 to 1888, nickel plated with gold wash and mother-of-pearl grips. Collection: Vic Williams.

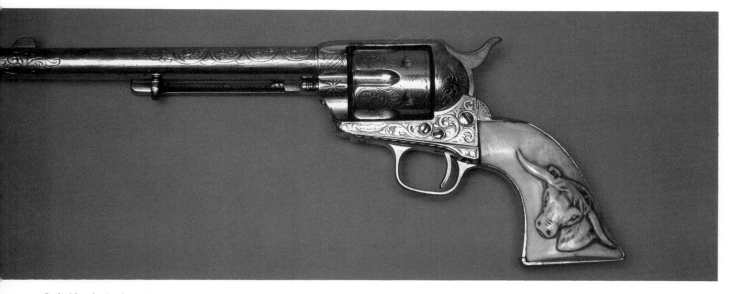

Colt Single Action Army, .45 cal. pistol, serial #20746, circa 1875. It has fine scroll and border motifs with nickel finish. It was engraved by L.D. Nimschke and shipped to Schuyler, Hartley and Graham, N.Y.C., on Sept. 30, 1875. The one-piece, carved ivory, steerhead grips, while not original to the gun, are of the period and are very pleasing. Collection: Dominick Cervone.

Colt, Single Action Army revolver, Serial #88611, .44/40 caliber, 7½'', blue finish with bullhead carved grips. Fifty were shipped to Hartley & Graham, New York, NY, March 10, 1884. Collection: Enrique Guerra.

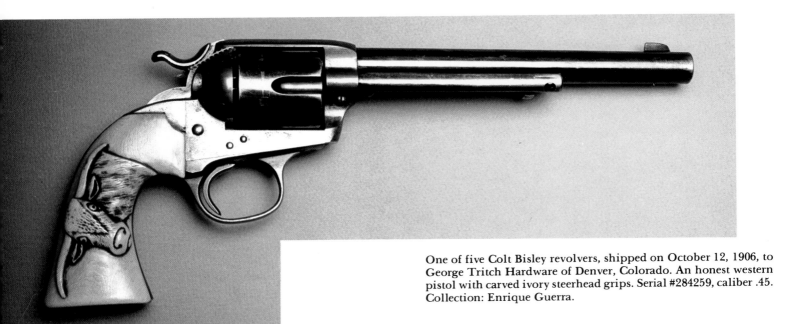

One of five Colt Bisley revolvers, shipped on October 12, 1906, to George Tritch Hardware of Denver, Colorado. An honest western pistol with carved ivory steerhead grips. Serial #284259, caliber .45. Collection: Enrique Guerra.

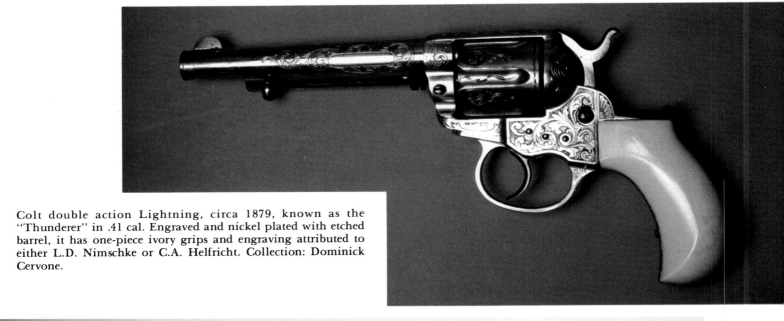

Colt double action Lightning, circa 1879, known as the "Thunderer" in .41 cal. Engraved and nickel plated with etched barrel, it has one-piece ivory grips and engraving attributed to either L.D. Nimschke or C.A. Helfricht. Collection: Dominick Cervone.

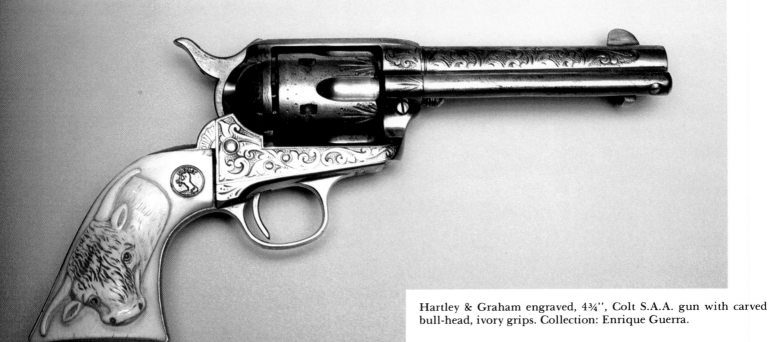

Hartley & Graham engraved, 4¾", Colt S.A.A. gun with carved bull-head, ivory grips. Collection: Enrique Guerra.

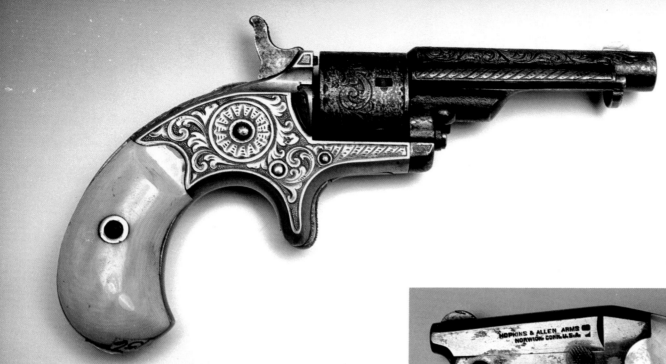

Colt New Line, open top, .22 caliber pistol. This gun features ivory grips and Nimschke engraving. Collection: Enrique Guerra.

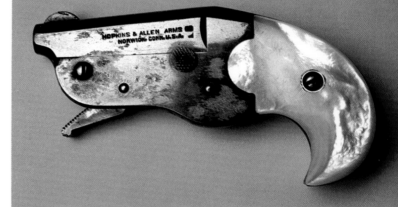

Hopkins & Allen Derringer .22 cal, blue with pearl grips. Collection: C.W. Lyle, Jr.

Chicago Palm pistol, serial number on the inside 10099, and 9349 on the revolving cylinders marked "Chicago Drum Co.—Chicago, Ill." Patented March 6, 1883. Collection: Dr James Brown.

Remington vest pocket single shot pistol set into a bible. Whether carried by a preacher or simply made for home protection, the owner of this outfit chose the page title "state and portion of the wicked, all alike in death" to inset his gun. Collection: Michael Friedman.

Portrait of a cowboy's gun. This Colt Peacemaker is a well worn but classic example of a sixshooter from the Old West. Manufactured in 1881 in .45 cal., (Serial #67400), it is engraved and has carved ivory grips. Collection: Michael Friedman.

Colt Single Action Army revolver with 7½" barrel and "B" style engraving, typical of the factory engraving in the 1874-1875 period. This gun may have been part of a military contract overrun, as there are ordnance department inspection marks present. Serial #14344, with ivory stocks. Collection: Thomas W. Connally.

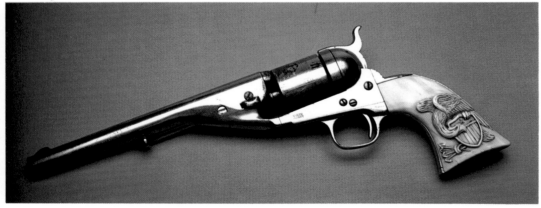

A Colt model 1861 Navy, with Richards-Mason conversion. This .38 caliber gun has American Eagle and shield carved ivory grips. Collection: C.W. Lyle, Jr.

Colt, Single Action, 45 cal, with 4¾" barrel, factory class C engraved, and shipped to Simmons Hardware Co., St. Louis in 1897. The carved pearl grips have the American eagle. The gun was ordered for a John Welch. Collection: Joe Gish.

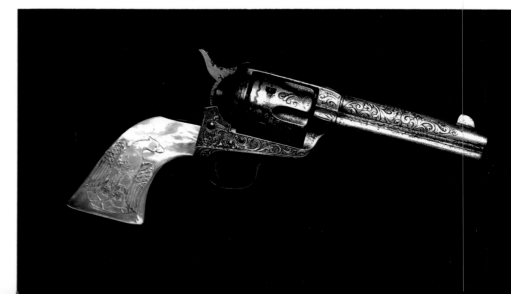

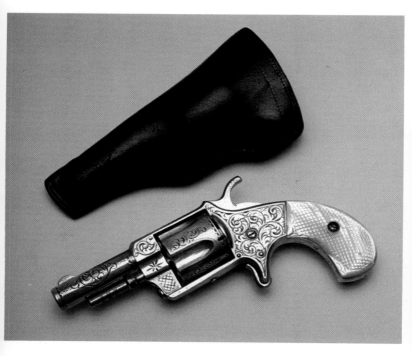

Rare Jacob Rupertus revolver, .41 rimfire, circa 1870s, in a silver-plated gold wash with checkered mother-of-pearl grips. It is factory engraved and shown with a form-fitted holster. Collection: Vic Williams.

A turn-of-the-entury stand for the Harrington & Richardson Arms Co. which were furnished to dealers as countertop display units. Collection: C.W. Lyle, Jr.

"Cloverleaf" revolver, circa 1871 to 1876, made by Bach of Hartford, Conn., 1½" barrel (rare), .41 cal., fine condition. Shown with a chamois purse holster. Collection: Vic Williams.

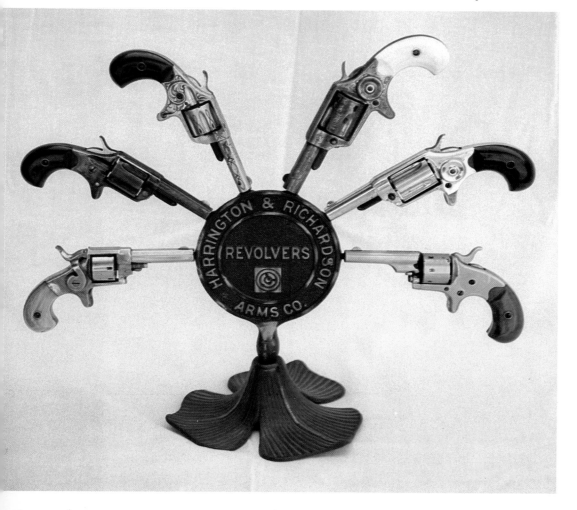

Rusty Relics

When one thinks of ancient artifacts, places like Greece or China might come to mind. Objects from past cultures which have been excavated and remain as silent reminders of the past. America too has it's artifacts but they are not ancient. In terms of the Old West, little in the way of historical relics have been uncovered; firstly because the period lasted only a short time and secondly because the West was so sparsely settled. Old horshoes, branding irons and arrowheads are not uncommon to find. But imagine unearthing a Colt Peacemaker frozen in time with its original cartridges still in the cylinder. Add to that the fact that the hammer was rusted tight in the cocked position and one of the cartridges had been spent. The impression is that this gun went down with it's owner in a gunfight and lay there for a hundred years before being re-discovered. Our imagination is encouraged to run wild. With each new "rusty relic" another great yarn can be envisioned.

For the western collector, the value of a rusty relic depends on its function, where it was found, and its state of preservation. Generally rust-outs are not costly when compared with normal antique guns, but their increase in popularity has made them both rarer and more desirable.

Colt S.A.A., .45 cal., rusted out, 7½" bbl, gun with original ivory grips. Completely frozen with rust and unloaded, this gun was dug up near Mexico City with another Colt Bisley .45 and a 4¾" Colt .45, all wrapped in a blanket. They were hidden hurriedly from Federal troops, according to the family, since these were illegally in the hands of civilians at the time. Collection: Dr. James Brown.

A Remington Army model, rusted out. This gun was found in Utah with some skeletal bones in a remote part of an old Indian territory on the "Jackass mail" route. A related story in the Salt Lake City newspaper reports that Indians killed the mail route driver approximately at the time the bones and gun date. Collection: Dr. James Brown.

The same Remington army model that was found in Utah, showing the gun fully loaded. Collection: Dr. James Brown.

Colt 1851 Navy revolver, circa 1850-1873. This percussion revolver was manufactured in Colt's Hartford factory but was a popular gun in the Old West until the S.A.A. was introduced in 1873. Collection: Michael Friedman.

Colt Model 1877 "lightning" .38 cal. double action revolver, excavated in Texas with 5 of its 6 chambers loaded. Collection: Michael Friedman.

This Remington New Model Army revolver was found about 90 years ago at a city dump in Fort Worth, Texas. Inside grip bears the notation "cabeza de vaca." Collection: Michael Friedman.

A homemade primitive weapon incorporating a firearm and a knife. It required a fuse to ignite and could have been prison made. 19th century. Collection: Michael Friedman.

Almost unrecognizable, this .44 cal. Smith & Wesson single action revolver has been frozen into a solid block of iron. Circa 1870s. Collection: Michael Friedman.

Rifles

Along with Samuel Colt there is only one man whose name is immediately recognizable in terms of the guns of the Old West, and that is Oliver Winchester. Like Colt, Winchester developed a firearm that was strong, durable, easy to load and most important, one that would repeat. The lever action repeating rifle probably had as great an impact on the Old West as any other single gun, including the Colt Single Action Army revolver. Both were dubbed "the guns that won the West" and for the entire second half of the 19th century, Winchesters were the rifles of choice among both cowboys and Indians (when they could get them). The following photos illustrate the various models that were in use during this period.

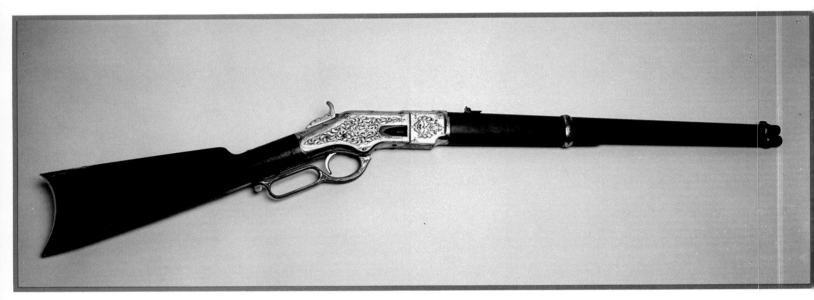

1866 Winchester carbine of special order and engraved for a customer from the Republic of Chile. Collection: Enrique Guerra.

The buffalo hunters didn't wash, and looked like animals. They dressed in strong, heavy, warm clothes and never changed them. You would see three or four of them walk up to a bar, reach down inside their clothes and see who could catch the first louse for the drinks. They were lousy and proud of it.

The cowpunchers was a totally different class from these other fellows on the frontier. We was the salt of the earth, anyway in our own estimation, and we had the pride that went with it. That was why Miles City changed so much after the trail herds got there; even the women changed. Because buffalo hunters and that kind of people would sleep with women that cowpunchers would'nt even look at, and it was on our account that they started bringing in girls from eastern cities, young girls and pretty ones. Those girls followed us up, like I told you, and we would meet old pals in new places.

But I missed out. There was one of those girls named Lily Davis, who was in Lincoln the winter and spring of '82, and I spent most of that winter staying in town with her. I really thought a lot of her—she was awfully kind and jolly and a good sout-didn't try to work you out of every damn cent you had. Next year she and her girl friend turned up in Cheyenne, and from there I heard they went to the Black Hills. They came to Miles City in '83, but Lily left before I got there and went to Butte. I never saw her again.

We Pointed Them North

Winchester Henry rifle which was presented to John Cox, a signer of the Act of Cessesion from the Union for the state of Texas, circa 1861. Collection: Enrique Guerra.

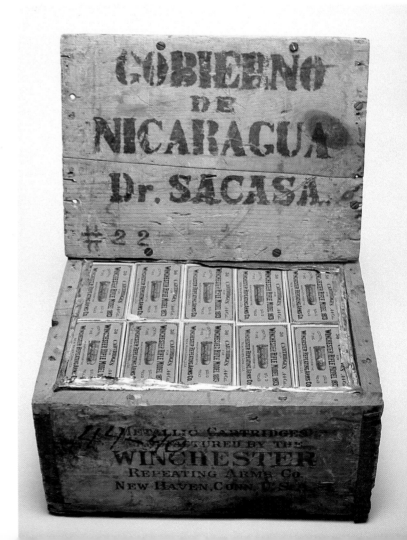

Complete case of Winchester .44-40 ammunition. 40 boxes. Original destination to the Nicaraguan Army. They had Winchester model 1873 muskets. Collection: Enrique Guerra.

Henry Repeating Rifle, serial #7558. .44 cal. rimfire. Designed by Benjamin Henry and manufactured by the New Haven Arms Company. Under Oliver Winchester's direction, the Henry Repeating Rifle was the first practical magazine-fed, breech-loading, repeating firearm. Initially rejected by the U.S. Army, this rifle later proved its superiority in the Civil War. Production lasted from 1860 to 1866, and some 13,000 were made. Collection: Thomas W. Connally.

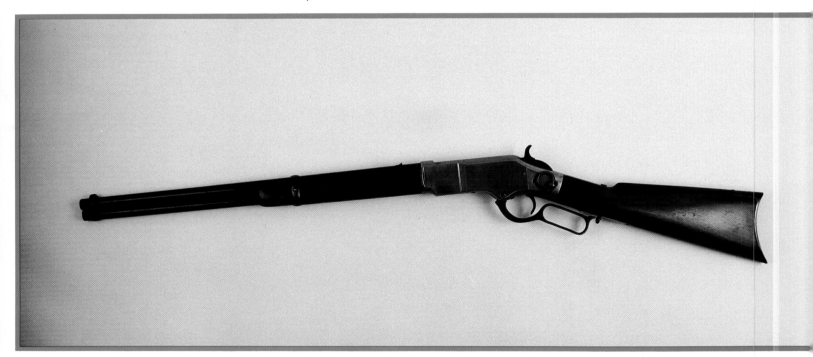

Winchester Model 1866, serial #121694 saddle ring carbine. Because of its brass receiver, this gun was affectionately named by Indians "Yellow Boy" and was a favorite among both cowboys and Indians. The successor to the Henry, the Model 1866, contained a major improvement by substituting the muzzle charge cap to a slot-in-the-side loading gate, making loading easier and faster. Total production 170,101. Collection: Thomas W. Connally.

Winchester Model 1873 saddle ring carbine, serial #16826, 20" barrel. Known as "the gun that won the West," the '73 Winchester was especially popular on the frontier due to the fact that its .44-40 ammunition was interchangeable with the Colt Frontier Six-Shooter. This model also had a much improved mechanism to previous models and resulted in a production of over 700,000, spanning fifty years. Collection: Thomas W. Connally.

Winchester Model 1873 rifle with round 24" barrel, serial #291099B. The first model 1873s were produced with an iron frame, but were later replaced by steel—as in this example. This resulted in both lower production costs and a lighter gun. The Model '73 is the most famous of all Winchesters and was the title of a movie starring James Stewart. Collection: Thomas W. Connally.

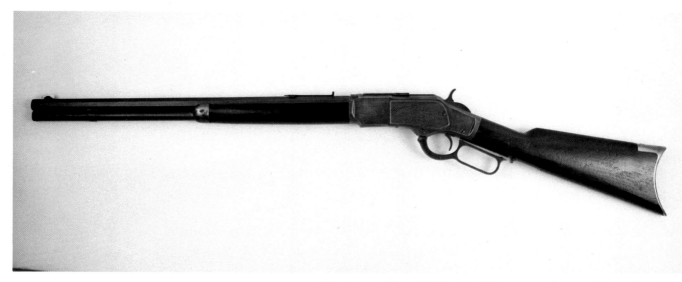

Winchester Model 1873 with 20" octagonal, smooth bore barrel. Smooth bore barrels were used by trick shooters and this rifle was apparently used by one of the best. Inscribed on the receiver is the name "Annie Oakley." Serial #356697B, .44 cal. Collection: Thomas W. Connally.

Winchester Model 1876. 40-60 cal. Serial #48128. Round, 28" barrel. Often referred to as the "Centennial Model." Winchester introduced the Model 1876 after many people called for a more powerful successor to the popular Model 1873. Production lasted until 1897, with a total of just over 63,000 being made. Collection: Thomas W. Connally.

Winchester Model 1892 rifle with a 24" octagonal barrel. Serial #412611. More than one million Model '92s were produced between 1892 and 1941. This model was designed to be the successor to the Model 1873. Collection: Thomas W. Connally.

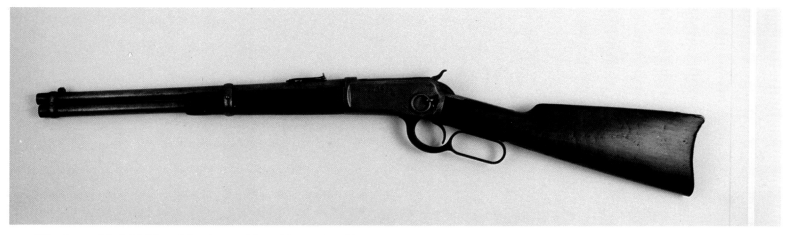

Winchester Model 1892 saddle ring carbine "Trapper" with 16" round barrel. Serial #57417. The diminuitive "trapper" model is both scarce and desirable among collectors. Collection: Thomas W. Connally.

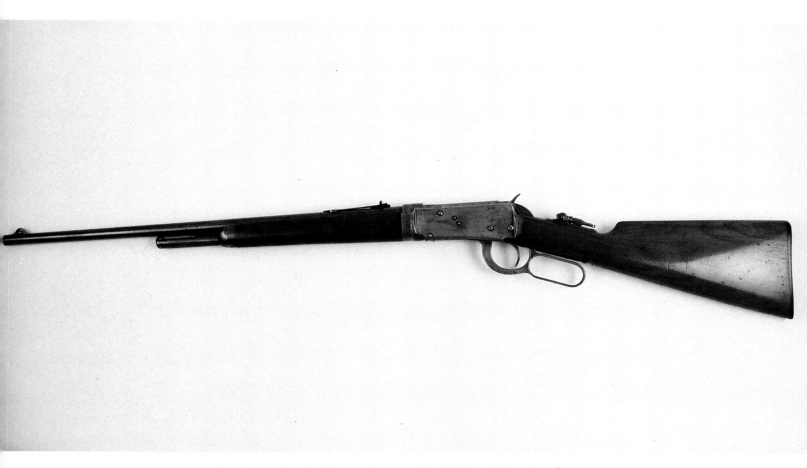

Winchester Model 1892 take down, serial #66019, 22" barrel and tang sight, cal. .30. W.C.F. This rifle breaks down into a very compact unit for traveling and is less common than rifles or carbines. Collection: Thomas W. Connally.

Colt Lightning slide action rifle, 24" octagonal barrel and .32 WCF, serial #9116. Colt introduced this model in 1884 and continued to manufacture it until 1902 with a total quantity of 89,777. Made in a variety of calibers, it shared chamberings with both the Single Action Army and the Double Action 1878 Frontier revolvers. Collection: Thomas W. Connally.

Chapter Twelve

Bowie Knives

Mexican dagger, circa 1890. The snake motif is made of silver and gold mounted on steel. Collection: Enrique Guerra.

Bone handled dirk or dagger with mother-of-pearl inlays and original sheath. This style of blade was used for "stabbing," not hunting or carving, and was typical of the type used by gamblers in the Old West. 5" blade signed "Henry Hobson." Collection: Thomas W. Connally.

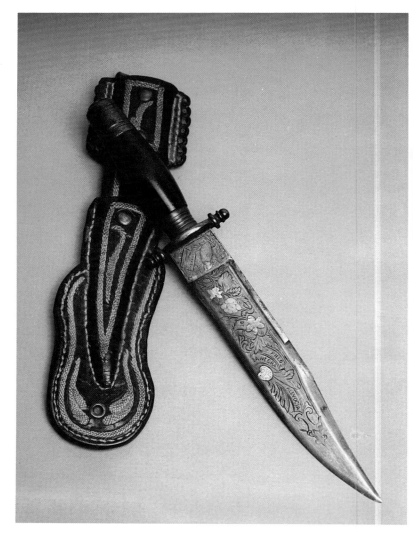

Mexican Bowie knife with a steel blade inlaid with gold and silver, ebony handle, dated "1810", and the owner's name on the blade. The original embroidered scabbard remains. Collection: Enrique Guerra.

Bowie knife with an English Sheffield blade and silver handle, hilt and sheath, made in Mexico, circa 1865, in fine condition. Collection: Enrique Guerra.

Mexican Bowie knife with a blade made in Sheffield, England and silver and gold intertwining snakes on the handle, circa 1850s to 1860s. Collection: Enrique Guerra.

Fancy little pearl handled knife with 6″ blade, carrying the etched inscription "Sure Defence." Collection: Thomas W. Connally.

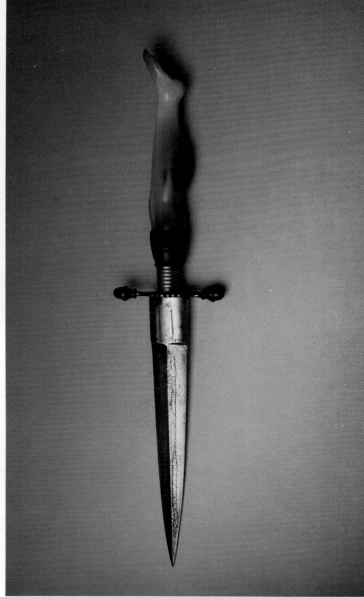

Unusual gentlman's dirk with a carved horn handle in the shape of a lady's leg, 19th century. Collection: C.W. Lyle, Jr.

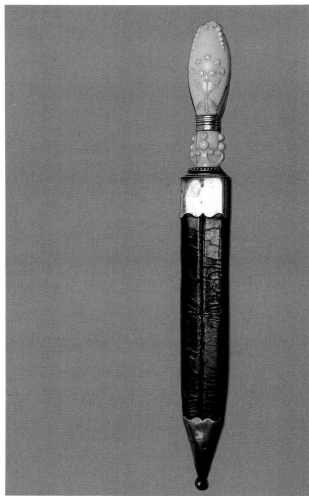

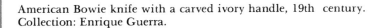

American Bowie knife with a carved ivory handle, 19th century. Collection: Enrique Guerra.

Mexican Bowie knife with a fine silver inlaid handle, marked "M-5-62" (meaning May 5, 1862). This knife belonged to Ignacis Laragosa Sequin, the commanding officer of the Mexican Army that defeated the French Foreign Legion at Puebla, Mexico. (French intervention Maximilian period), circa 1862. Maker unknown, but probably made at Amococ Puebla. Collection: Enrique Guerra.

Rare Mexican dagger made from a bayonet, circa 1860, with a steel sheath, silver trim, and an exquisite carved bone handle depicting the Mexican Eagle. Collection: Enrique Guerra.

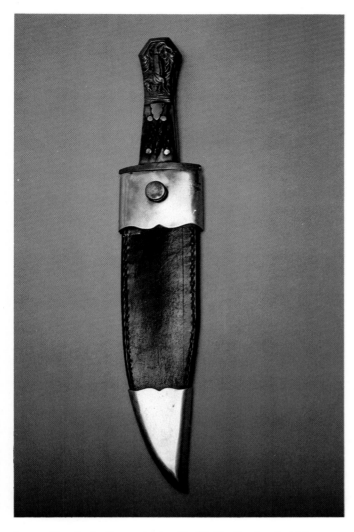

Large Bowie knife made in Sheffield, England, 19th century. Collection: Enrique Guerra.

Brass carborundum advertising whetstone. Large stag handled folding knife by Richmond Works, Sheffield, England. Small folding knife by John Milner & Co., Sheffield, England. Collection: C.W. Lyle, Jr.

Unusual signed American Bowie knife with stag handle by Edward Barnes, 19th century. Collection: Enrique Guerra.

Giant bowie knife with stag handle. The sheath was made for this knife but was probably done later. Guard and blade appear to be Mexican. 19th century. Collection: Michael Friedman.

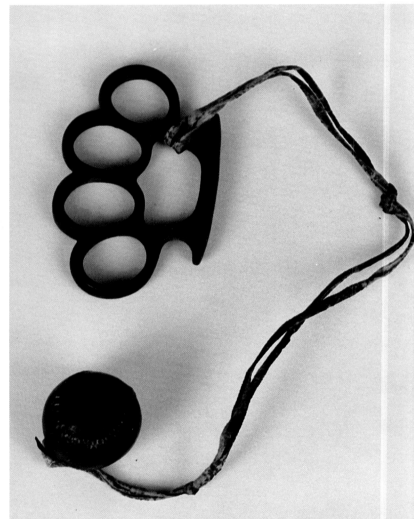

This unusual set of knuckles has been modified by its owner to give an added edge against an adversary. The leather covered ball is lead filled and attached by a rawhide thong. Double trouble, circa 1890. Collection: Michael Friedman.

Jail house lock, circa late 1800s, from Paradise, Texas. Collection: Vic Williams.

Collection of knuckles.
Top: Carved wood - brass - brass (dated 5-12-1894)
Center: Brass - brass - iron (for a lady)
Bottom: Brass - nickel plated iron - iron
Collection: Vic Williams.

Assortment of knuckles which were popular from the 1880s to the
1930s. Collection: C.W. Lyle, Jr.

Hand cuffs: Right: Patented, July 17, 1866. The single lock was popular after the Civil War. Left: Typical early cuffs used by law enforcement officals in the West. Both have original keys. Collection: Vic Williams.

Hand cuffs: Right: Patented, May 2, 1899, with original key, nickle plated "Bean/Cobb." Left: Patented, July 4, 1899, with original key. A former owner's name, "T. Maxey" is engraved on the cuff. Collection: Vic Williams.

Hand cuffs. Bottom: A jug type manufactured by Marlin Firearms Co., of New Haven, Connecticut, patented December 2, 1879. Top: Manufactured by Mattatuck Mfg. Co., Waterbury, Conn. Patented in 1901. Note the trigger mechanism to facilitate application, its trade name was "The Maltby." Collection: Vic Williams.

Chapter Thirteen

Jewelry

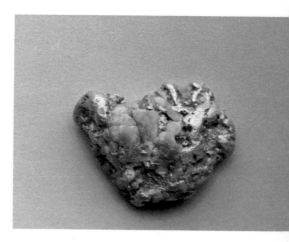

This super gold quartz nugget, weighing 2.605 oz. was found in the Yuba River area of California in the 1980s. Nuggets of this size (1 oz. or more) are rare. Collection: James H. MacKie.

Gold Quartz Jewelry

No single event had a greater impact on the settling of the West than did the California Gold Rush of 1849. While gold had been discovered in 1848, the news had no way of reaching the East. At that point the telegraph only existed in the East and it wasn't until President James Polk announced it's discovery in December of 1848 that people became excited. Almost overnight the country contracted "gold fever."

By ship or wagon train, the '49ers came by the thousands with wild dreams of untold riches just waiting there for the taking. Tangible goods in the Gold Rush region were very expensive because ships loaded with cargo had to travel from their eastern ports, around Cape Horn and up the California coast to San Francisco. From there equipment was transported by wagon or mule to the outlying areas. A barrel of flour could cost as much as $800, and one man reported that he had paid $11 for a jar of pickles. In 1850, these prices were staggering and for the vast majority, those who did not strike it rich, life was very hard indeed.

But there were a few who became rich. Gold quartz jewelry, probably the most desirable of all antiques from the Gold Rush Era are magnificent items of jewelry fashioned from quartz with veins of gold running through them. The quartz was found in many colors, but more often than not there was little visible gold. Occasionally quartz with large and distinct veins of gold would surface and be chosen for use in jewelry. Due to the fragile nature of this stone, much was lost to breakage while being made into jewelry. Nowhere else, and at no other time, were such pieces produced. Master jewelers fashioned some of the most beautiful jewelry of the Victorian period, including pocket watches, brooches, fobs and chains, earrings, lockets, rings from gold quartz.

Tri-colored gold quartz match safe with a diamond pattern on one side, candy stripes on the reverse, and the sides and top covered in gold quartz, inscribed "Moses from Henry. Birthday Oct 3rd 1875," 1⅜" X 2¼". Collection: Sandra & Ronald Van Anda.

Gold miner's pocket scales in original marked tin container, circa 1849. Collection: Roger Baker.

Match safe with gold quartz top and oval front, circa 1870s, probably made by Shreve & Co., San Francisco, California. Collection: James H. MacKie.

Finely engraved gold quartz match safe in excellent condition. Circa 1870-1880. Collection: Roger Baker.

Tri-colored gold quartz match safe with 53 pieces of gold quartz and 4 pieces of agate covering the front, back, top, and sides, circa 1870s, 2½" x 1⅜". Collection: Sandra & Ronald Van Anda.

Gold quartz match safe with a diamond on one side and a large piece of white quartz on reverse, inscribed "H.C.R. from E.C," 1⅜" x 2¼". Collection: Sandra & Ronald Van Anda.

Gold quartz match safe, circa 1870 to 1880. Collection: C.W. Lyle, Jr.

Among the major jewelery houses in San Francisco was George C. Shreve & Co., which was founded in 1852 and is still in business today. Other names associated with this type of jewelry are Barrett and Sherwood, Rothchild and Hadenfeld, and Abram Andrews' Diamond Palace. By the end of the 19th century, but certainly by the time of the great California earthquake, little if any of this jewelry was still being made. Major pieces have for the most part been collected and are now in private hands or museums. However, smaller but still very beautiful pieces are still turning up. Not just in California, as visitors to the west between 1850 and 1900 brought many pieces back to their homes in the East. Therefore, while great examples of this work are relatively rare, there is a chance of running across these little treasures in the most unlikely places. Since this is a little known specialty, gold quartz jewelry tends to be undervalued by antiques dealers outside of California.

Very rare watch fob in the form of a safe, approx. 1¼'' high x ⅞'' wide x ¾'' deep. The top is divided into two equal panels of white gold quartz and agate. One side is black gold quartz and turquoise with a matrix. The other side is white gold quartz and azurite/ malachite. Back is gray gold quartz and dendritic (moss) agate. The telescoping safe doors are engraved with butterflies, flowers and geometric design and the door latch slides to unlock additional doors which enclose ore samples. The wheels are moveable. Collection: Sandra & Ronald Van Anda.

Unusual gold quartz watch chain in which four pieces of gold quartz and three other stones dangle from a horseshoe, with filigree initials "HCR". Collection: Sandra & Ronald Van Anda.

Tri-colored gold quartz butterfly of black, white and pink quartz, 3'' x 1½'', which was made in San Francisco, circa 1870s. Collection: Sandra & Ronald Van Anda.

Gold quartz watch fob with ore samples in the center and a photo locket on the reverse, 1¾'' x 1¼''. Collection: Ronald & Sandra Van Anda.

A newly mined gold quartz specimen, cut and polished, as found in Mariposa, California. Cracks and breaks in the raw quartz caused craftsmen many problems in making this type of jewelry. Collection: James H. MacKie.

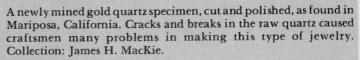

Indian-head, five-dollar gold piece with a rare gold quartz pocket watch and linked chain, circa 1870 to 1880. Collection: C.W. Lyle, Jr.

Watch chains with gold matrix quartz were found in a wide range of sizes and designs. Collection: Roger Baker.

Beautiful pair of gold quartz cuff links, circa 1870 to 1880. Collection: C.W. Lyle, Jr.

Very fine 3-color gold watch, watch chain and fob with gold quartz stones. Collection: Sandra and Ronald Van Anda.

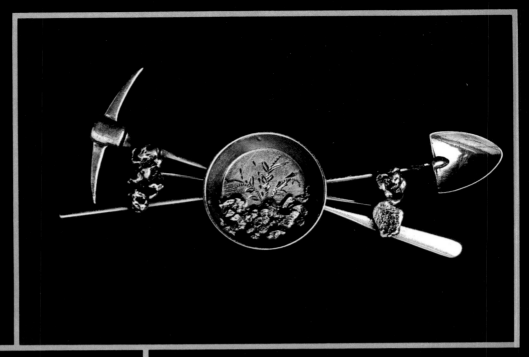

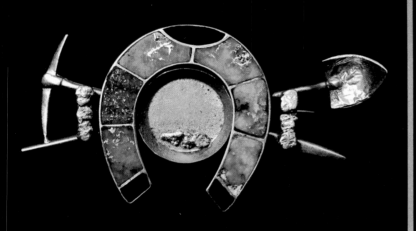

Gold rush jewelry also was made in plain gold without quartz, like this gold brooch. Some of these designs were made again during the 1890s Alaska Gold Rush. Collection: Roger Baker.

Two brooches depicting miner's tools. Collection: Roger Baker.

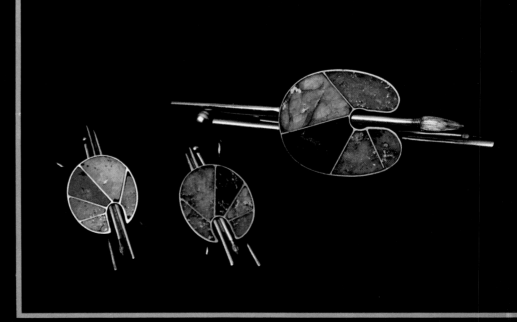

These matching earrings and brooch use different colors of quartz on the artist's palate. Collection: Roger Baker.

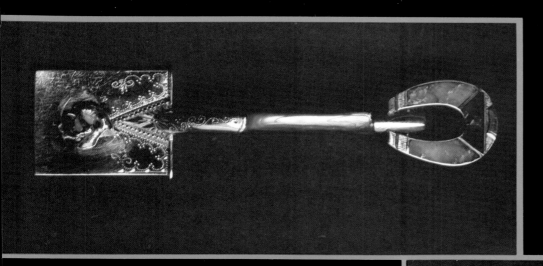

Ladies' brooches were sometimes purchased by miners as souvenirs for wives and daughters back home. Collection: Roger Baker.

Gold quartz pendant or watch fob with a diamond (original box). Collection: Roger Baker.

Cane heads of gold quartz were produced by 1854 and perhaps even earlier. The crown or top of this cane is faceted like a diamond and surrounded by eight cabochons of different colored quartz. It was a presentation piece of exceptional quality. Collection: Roger Baker.

Silver money clip with gold flowers and ruby insets, a double headed eagle, and 32nd Degree Masonic emblems, circa 1920s to 1930s. Collection: C.W. Lyle, Jr.

Gold and silver quartz pocket knife with samples of gold encasing one side, marked "H.A.L. Miller, San Francisco." Collection: Sandra & Ronald Van Anda.

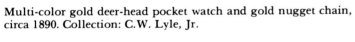

Multi-color gold deer-head pocket watch and gold nugget chain, circa 1890. Collection: C.W. Lyle, Jr.

Sterling silver cigar cutter. Circa 1890-1900. Collection: C.W. Lyle, Jr.

Rare and very fine, size 16, four-color 14kt gold watch featuring a
train, circa 1890, made by Elgin Watch Co., Elgin, Illinois.
Collection: Brad Witherell.

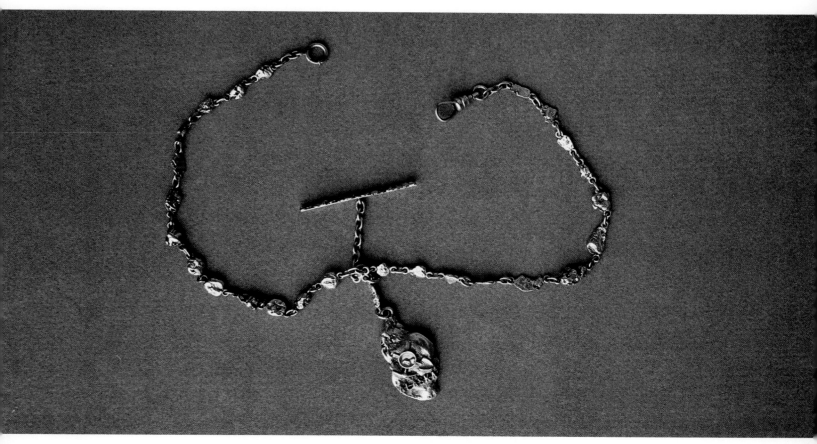

Gold nugget watch chain with a large (1 oz.) gold nugget from
Alaska, total wt. 3 oz., circa 1890 to 1900, from Juneau, Alaska.
Collection: James H. MacKie.

A 14kt gold watch, engraved with an Indian scene, size 16, circa 1882, was made by the Elgin Watch Co., of Elgin, Illinois. Collection: James H. MacKie.

This horseshoe-shaped money clip is sterling silver with gold nails. Collection: Roger Baker.

Presentation medal made of enamel, gold and diamond. Collection: Roger Baker.

Beautiful multi-color 14kt gold watch, size 18, with eight diamonds in a horse and horseshoe design, circa 1889, made by Waltham Watch Co. of Elizabeth, N.J. Collection: Brad Witherell.

Three-color 14k gold ring from the 1890s Alaskan Yukon Territory Gold Rush. Collection: James MacKie.

Watch fob with diamond inset on gold nugget. Circa 1880-1890. Collection: James Mackie.

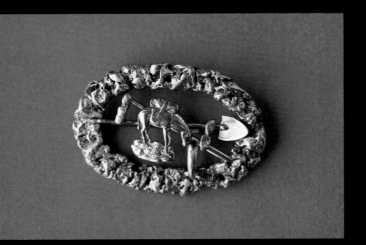

Gold Rush brooch comprised of gold nuggets. Pins such as this were often purchased by lucky miners and sent to loved ones back home. Circa 19th century. Collection: Roger Baker.

A superb French enamel matchsafe from the mid-1800s. Slave scenes were popular even if they were in bad taste. Collection: Roger Baker.

An advertising match safe for Thornes whiskey, circa 1890s. Collection: C.W. Lyle, Jr.

A figural matchsafe in the shape of a pair of overalls. Collection: C.W. Lyle, Jr.

Brass matchsafes depicting a hatching duck and a cat and mouse. Collection: C.W. Lyle, Jr.

Matchsafes

A group of Indianhead match safes. Collection: Roger Baker.

Chapter Fourteen

Saloon

The Old West was for the most part a society of men. Few women dared or desired to venture into the environment of frontier life. There were few amenities and little female companionship. San Francisco was a notable exception because of the great influx of people seeking their fortune in the California gold fields in the 1850s. Towns sprang up and disappeared overnight as news of new strikes spread. It would be ten to fifteen years before the rest of the Old West began to resemble the towns and cities we see depicted in the movies. The gold rush provided great opportunity and wealth to San Francisco. Opulent furnishings arrived by ship from the East and even from Europe as competition for the miners' gold grew. In California cities such as San Francisco, Sacramento, Eureka, and Bodie, the saloon was the very center of activity where one could get news, libation, companionship, gambling and in some cases even a haircut. The same was true later in cow towns throughout the West, but on a much smaller scale. Since saloons were generally the first business to open, often they began in tents and later moved to wooden buildings like those we all know from the movies.

BACK BARS

In the early days of the gold rush period, whiskey and rum were transported to California from the East by ship. From their western ports, distributors transported heavy oak casks by rough trails to saloons throughout the gold country. Saloon keepers transferred the contents into bottles (known as Back Bar bottles) which were given to saloons by the distilleries and distributors. Sometimes very elaborate, these bottles are early examples of direct marketing. Since there was probably little difference between one brand of Kentucky mash and another, one way to obtain brand preference and loyalty was to create a beautiful and sophisticated back bar bottle. Made to look like fancy decanters of cut crystal, back bar bottles came in a few different basic styles. 1. The most common was the "fifth" or quart bottle with white enamel lettering depicting the name of the manufacturer. 2. Another fairly common bottle style has an etched label on which the company name is cut into the glass and gold filled. 3. Bottles with four color enamel labels are quite rare and desirable and often have an artistic representation combined with white enamel lettering. 4. The final

While decanter-style bar bottles with glass labels are scarce, none are harder to find than those with the distributor's name. This one says "Meyerfield and Gant, Portland, Oregon," circa 1890. Collection: Roger Baker.

Opposite page:
Trade tokens from the latter part of the 19th century, made from nickel, brass, copper and aluminum. In earlier days a nickel bought a glass of beer and two bits (25 cents) purchased two shots of hard liquor. Collection: C.W. Lyle, Jr.

> *a Lot of saloon men and tinhorn gamblers bit the dust. While I saw several shooting scrapes in saloons and sporting houses, I never saw a man shot dead, though some died afterwards.*
>
> *We Pointed Them North*

One of the prettier white enamel, lettered back bar decanters, circa 1890. Collection: Cathy and Gene Gavin.

Although technically a white enamel bottle, the name and location make it rare and very special, circa 1880s to 1890s. Collection: Roger Baker.

Unusual twisted, glass back bar bottle with gold lettering, circa 1890. Collection: Cathy and Gene Gavin.

Although technically a white enamel bottle, the name makes this one special, circa 1880s to 1890s. Collection: Roger Baker.

Enameled bar bottles are found in three variations, as illustrated here: 1. Multi-colored lettering appears on Canada Rye, 2. Full color scene on the Mammoth Cave, and, 3. Plain white lettering on the Gold Dust. Collection: Roger Baker.

category can only be described as very rare and very desirable. These are label-under-glass bottles, formed with a depression matching the size of the label. A thin piece of glass with a color decal applied to the underside is set into the recessed area and affixed with bees wax. The appearance resembles a picture inside the glass. Produced both as generic bottles and those for specific distilleries, they represent the ultimate in Back Bar collecting. Because they were more difficult and expensive to produce, fewer of them have survived. Additionally, the thin glass label made them more fragile than the other types of bottles. The most desirable label-under-glass bottles depict pretty ladies and advertising.

Back Bar bottles are not the only saloon-related antiques. Other items, such as gambling accoutrements, of value and quality that might have appeared in a 19th century western saloon are collectible and will be shown in subsequent chapters.

Baker's Choice whiskey is decorated on the same cut glass bottle as the Old Durham. It appears that most bar bottles were produced or custom made by only a few manufacturers. Collection: Roger Baker.

Lavish use of color and a huge label decorate this Yellowstone bar bottle. A cut neck adds to the unusual appeal of this hard-to-find piece. Collection: Roger Baker.

"Suspects His Master". Collection: Roger Baker.

Reflecting the popularity of hunting at the turn of the century, the Old Scenter made a fine back bar presence. Collection: Roger Baker.

This unusual bottle has a cut neck and a multi-colored enamel label. Collection: Roger Baker.

Hard to find colored enamel pinch bottles in excellent condition.
Collection: Roger Baker.

Custer's Reserve was a San Francisco brand whiskey. This colored enamel bottle is circa 1890 to 1900. Collection: Roger Baker.

The Five Jacks image on this decanter for Michelson's Whiskey is almost identical to the image on the Five Jacks pinch bottle. This bottle is desirable to both saloon and gambling collectors. Collection: Roger Baker.

Old Government is another San Francisco bottle which has been found with slight variations in the colored label as well as white enamel and gold lettering. Collection: Roger Baker.

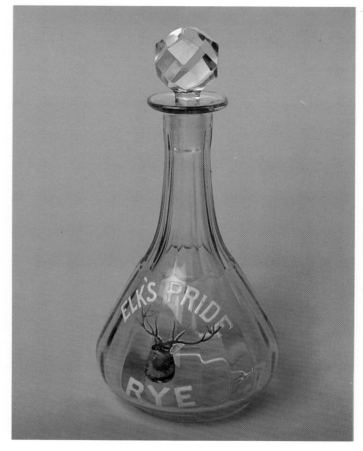

Elk were popular design motifs in advertising at the turn of the century and were featured on many bar bottles, trays, signs, etc. Collection: Roger Baker.

Label under glass "Pretty Girl" back bar bottle. Circa 1890. Collection: Roger Baker.

Gold Dust Whiskey was a well-known San Francisco brand which capitalized on the gold rush history. This ½ gal. oversized bottle was probably used as a display or advertising piece, circa 1895 to 1900. It is a fine bottle in nice condition. Collection: Roger Baker.

This port bottle features one of the risqué ladies with a plunging neckline. Absolutley scandalous in Victorian times, it was good merchandising in the saloons of the Old West, circa 1880s to 1890s. Collection: Roger Baker.

Label under glass "Pretty Girl" saloon bottle. Circa 1890.
Collection: Roger Baker.

This group of five back bar bottles picture each of the ladies
apparently offered in this set. They are among the most colorful and
pretty of all that were made. These are approximately 5th size
bottles, circa 1890 to 1905. Collection: Roger Baker.

A lime squeezer made of rosewood and ivory was a unique San Francisco design. Squeezers were popular to make "punch" with fruit juices. They were available from Will and Finck, M. Price and J.H. Shintz. Collection: Roger Baker.

Large label-under-glass display bottles which advertise liquor are very rare. This is one of the more graphic examples. One-half gallon size. Collection: Roger Baker.

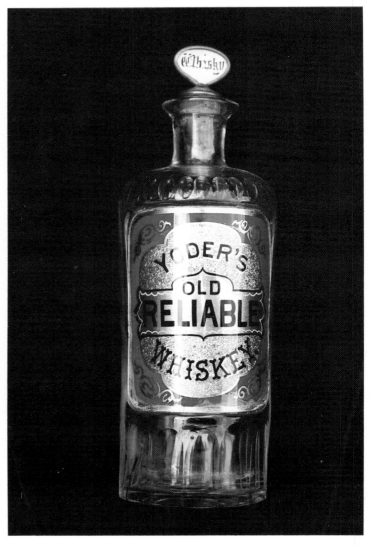

Unusual label-under-glass back bar bottle in fine condition, circa 1890. Collection: Michael Friedman.

Detail of left photo lime squeezer.

Both of these bottles were custom-made and are unique. Collection: Roger Baker.

This group of four flasks all were made for San Francisco saloons in a bottle style which appears to be unique to San Francisco advertising flasks. Collection: Roger Baker.

This race horse image appears on several label-under-glass bottles but none were better than this rare, old San Francisco brand. Collection: Roger Baker.

An old Swan bottle which pictures Lotta Crabtree, the Swedish nightingale. She was popular worldwide but especially revered in San Francisco. Collection: Roger Baker.

This Old Swan decanter shows a fanciful cupid riding a swan as its brand identification. Collection: Roger Baker.

This round decanter seems to have been used exclusively for Western- or San Francisco-based companies. Pioneer whiskey is one of a half dozen variations known. Collection: Roger Baker.

This advertising mug for Anhaeuser Busch, is in near-mint condition. The company dominated the Western and San Francisco markets well before the turn of the century. Collection: Roger Baker.

Marie Antoinette proves that not all mugs were for advertising beer. All of these mugs are the oversized ½-gallon variety. Collection: Roger Baker.

Jacob Ruppert is another standard mug with a custom glass label. Collection: Roger Baker.

These are known as "Good for" mirrors which served as trade tokens for saloons. They had a value, usually, of one drink—either worth 10 or 12½ cents. The state of origin and image determined the desirability of these mirrors. They are all scarce except the Raymonds Hotel mirrors. (Mirror on reverse side). Collection: Roger Baker.

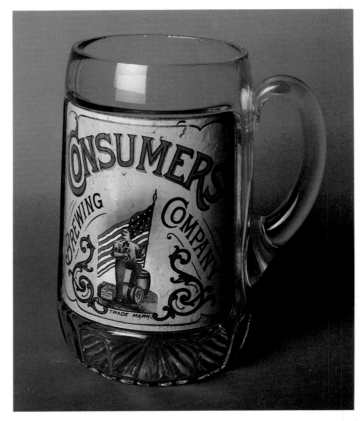

This half-gallon size mug is another advertising display piece with a label-under-glass feature. The example is very scarce since most have cracks or damage from being banged against other bar bottles. This one is no exception, approximately 12" tall and 8" wide. Collection: Roger Baker.

Glass labeled flasks were popular souvenir items at G.A.R. (Grand Army of the Republic) conventions. The oval flask, dated 1895, depicts the GAR medal and advertises I.W. Harper whiskey. The Dewey flask probably dates 1898-99 and celebrates Admiral Dewey's heroism in the Spanish-American war. The flags and medal version is from about the same period. While not rare, these are hard to find in nice condition. Collection: Roger Baker.

This flask has it all: Lady Liberty, the Shield, American Eagle, the Constitution and the Nations Capital. They combine to make this one of the finest flasks. This image also appeared on a round flask. Collection: Roger Baker.

This gambler's pocket flask with card faces is another type of bottle utilizing the label-under-glass method. Scarce, it dates circa 1890. Collection: Roger Baker.

Pretty ladies in near mint condition on canteen style flasks. This style appeared at the turn of the century. Collection: Roger Baker.

Humerous subjects in good condition such as these are hard to find
and very desirable. Collection: Roger Baker.

A group of lady flasks with glass label images, the most popular and
most valuable. Collection: Roger Baker.

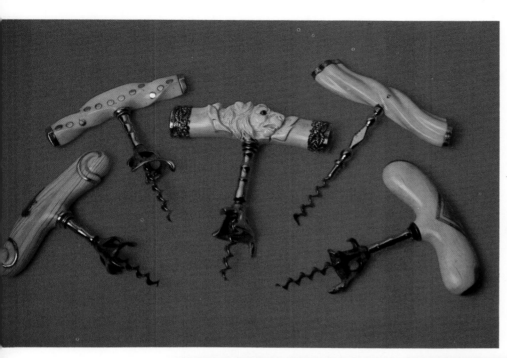

A variety of American, carved, ivory-handled corkscrews of the late Victorian era. Collection: Roger Baker.

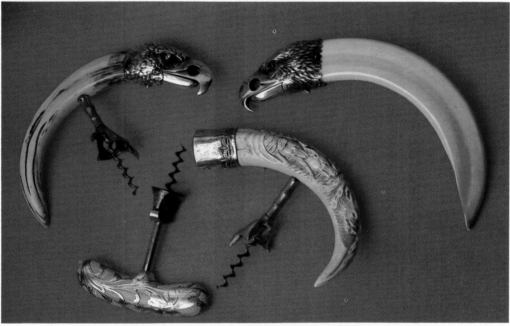

The large cigar cutters have eagle heads in two different versions; the heads are different and one is fitted with a corkscrew. American, circa 1890. Collection: Roger Baker.

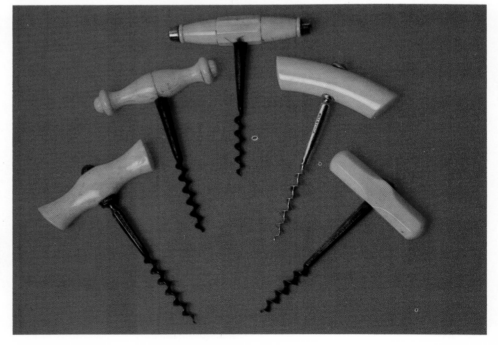

Group of ivory-handled corkscrews made in San Francisco during the gold rush era. The makers are, left to right: Will & Finck, Will & Finck, M. Price, Will & Finck and Haviland (made by Will & Finck). Collection: Roger Baker.

These whiskey glasses in colored enamel are uncommon. The two on the ends feature war heros of the Spanish-American war. The center glass is earlier and depicts a Tarot card. Collection: Roger Baker.

Fine pair of silver coated back bar bottles with white enamel lettering. Circa 1890. Collection: Cathy and Gene Gavin.

Wunder Brewing, with red letters, is a scarce San Francisco brand that expired with the earthquake and fire (1906). Two Drinks is a 2-bit (double) shot glass. American Club and Old Windsor are white enamel and less common than the etched glass. Collection: Roger Baker.

Whiskey glass with a self-explanatory message. Collection: C.W. Lyle, Jr.

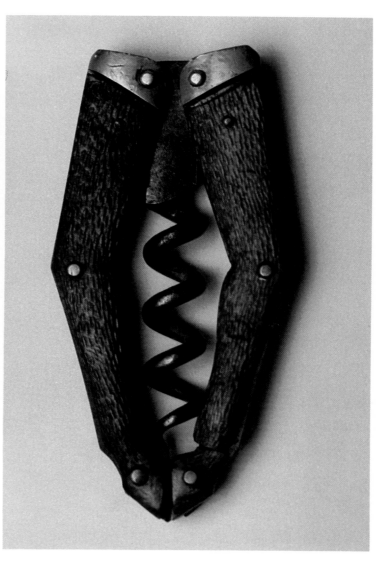

Very unusual, horse-leg, celluloid, folding corkscrew, circa 1890s. Collection: C.W. Lyle, Jr.

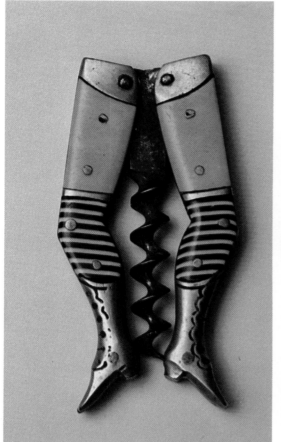

A folding, lady-leg corkscrew of celluloid. Collection: C.W. Lyle, Jr.

Unusual 19th century spitoon in the image of a stylized turtle. Stepping on its head caused its lid to open on its back. Collection: Vic Williams.

On this scarce, matching pair of bottles, the flowers are applied lithographs while everything else is hand painted. Collection: Roger Baker.

Kellerstrass Belle of Missouri is lavishly decorated with hand-painted flowers and rye stalks completely covering the bottle. Few bar bottles had such extensive art work. Collection: Roger Baker.

This Keiser Bar bottle appears to show a celebration of the fourth of July or perhaps the anniversary of the great earthquake. It is also one of the few made for a specific saloon and is one of the earliest label-under-glass bottles. The decoration pokes fun at Horace Greely whose bare bottom is exposed. The caption reads, "What Greely knows about corn." His anti-alcohol crusade earned him the wrath of the distillery industry. Collection: Roger Baker.

Pages 204 & 205, 1st row, left to right:
Label-under-glass, 5th-size bottle which depicts one of the five stock "Pretty Ladies."

It is hard to imagine a more Western image than that of the Yellowstone Falls. This brand name was probably adopted at the time Yellowstone became a national park. Collection: Roger Baker.

Detail of label under glass back bar bottle. Circa 1890. Collection: Roger Baker.

Five Jacks Whiskey is one of the scarce colored enamel pinch bottles especially popular with bar bottle enthusiasts. It dates from about 1890 to 1905. Mammoth Cave is one of the more colorful enamel bottles. It, too, is scarce, probably used only for a few years before the reuse of bar bottles was prohibited by law in 1906. This Clark's Rye is another American brand which features a bold label on a pinch style bottle. Only a dozen variations of colored labeled pinches are known to exist. Collection: Roger Baker.

Label detail shows this bottle to be a Virginia brand, probably indicating a private label for a distributor. Collection: Roger Baker.

The Five Jacks image on this decanter for Michelson's Whiskey is almost identical to the image on the Five Jacks pinch bottle. This is a rare bottle, desirable to both saloon and gambling collectors. Collection: Roger Baker.

2nd row, left to right:
Five Jacks Whiskey is one of the scarce colored enamel pinch bottles especially popular with bar bottle enthusiasts. It dates from about 1890 to 1905. Mammoth Cave is one of the more colorful enamel bottles. It, too, is scarce, probably used only for a few years before the reuse of bar bottles was prohibited by law in 1906. This Clark's Rye is another American brand which features a bold label on a pinch style bottle. Only a dozen variations of colored labeled pinches are known to exist. Collection: Roger Baker.

The Rooster on this Chicken Cock decanter is another example of a bottle from one of the many unusual makers of Whiskey. This has more color than most and is scarce in both the pinch and the cylinder styles, while the Burwood Leopard With A Crown is not common, Burwood in white enamel on a regular quart style bar bottles is common. Collection: Roger Baker.

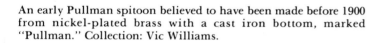

Painted trade sign. Collection: Allan Katz.

Advertising shot glasses marked "Grandpa's Rye Whiskey," circa 1890 to 1900. Collection: Vic Williams.

An early Pullman spitoon believed to have been made before 1900 from nickel-plated brass with a cast iron bottom, marked "Pullman." Collection: Vic Williams.

Some glass bottles were hand-made, hand-painted, or custom-made. Both of these are custom-made and are unique. Collection: Roger Baker.

Reflecting the popularity of hunting at the turn of the century, the Old Scenter made a fine back bar presence. Collection: Roger Baker.

Gold Dust Whiskey was a well-known San Francisco brand which capitalized on the gold rush history. This ½ gal. oversized bottle was probably used as a display or advertising piece, circa 1895 to 1900. It is a fine bottle in nice condition. Collection: Roger Baker.

Colored enamel labels such as these are found in some variety but are not common. The Sunny Brook is one of the few brand names that survived Prohibition, and it is more common than Old Prentice. Collection: Roger Baker.

3rd row, left to right:

The Baltimore address seen on this label indicates a distributor rather than a distiller. Many Eastern brands were supplied to the West by the transcontinental railroad that was completed in the late 1880s. Collection: Roger Baker.

This Keiser Bar bottle appears to show a celebration of the fourth of July or perhaps the anniversary of the great earthquake. It is also one of the few made for a specific saloon and is one of the earliest label-under-glass bottles known. The decoration pokes fun at Horace Greely whose bare bottom is exposed. The caption reads, "What Greely knows about corn." His anti-alcohol crusade earned him the wrath of the distillery industry. Collection: Roger Baker.

Detail of a colored enamel back bar bottle. Circa 1890. Collection: Roger Baker.

"Suspects His Master". Circa turn of the century. Collection: Roger Baker.

Five Jacks Whiskey is one of the scarce colored enamel pinch bottles especially popular with bar bottle enthusiasts. It dates from about 1890 to 1905. Mammoth Cave is one of the more colorful enamel bottles. It, too, is scarce, probably used only for a few years before the reuse of bar bottles was prohibited by law in 1906. This Clark's Rye is another American brand which features a bold label on a pinch style bottle. Only a dozen variations of colored labeled pinches are known to exist. Collection: Roger Baker.

A money box, circa late-1800s from an old saloon in Goldfield, Nevada. This was hand-made to hold silver coins, gold and paper money. Collection: Vic Wiliams.

Chapter Fifteen

Barber Shop

Next to the saloon, the barber shop was probably the most socially active establishment in town and was usually a cowboy's first stop when he came to town after days or weeks on the trail or range. Here he could get a shave, a haircut and even a tooth pulled. Often the barber was the closest thing to a doctor in an early frontier town. The barber shop was also a place to catch up on the news. Since sooner or later every man went there, the barber knew all the local gossip.

Most men who frequented a particular barber had their own shaving mug there. Each was personalized with the patron's name (generally in gold script). Some contained an artistic rendering such as flowers or a design, while others had decorations relating to the occupation of the patron. Occupational mugs were beautifully and elaborately painted and are highly prized. Those with unusual subjects in fine condition are rare and can be quite costly. The following examples represent some of the best.

Stock bottles were produced to accommodate custom labels. These are the glass label style. Collection: Roger Baker.

This personalized barber bottle has the name of its owner and a photograph of his son. Collection: Roger Baker.

Milk glass barber bottles were moulded in standard styles to be customized on order. Collection: Roger Baker.

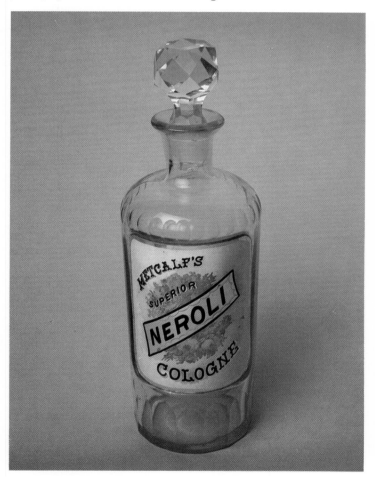

Metcalf's Neroli is a hand-painted, glass-label bottle, 11'' high, in mint condition and scarce. Collection: Roger Baker.

Customized or personalized bottles were few in number when compared to standard bottles. Even rarer are these near-mint condition label-under-glass bottles. Collection: Roger Baker.

Set of glass-label barber bottles in their original rack. Excellent condition. Circa 1870-80. Collection: Roger Baker.

Four straight razors with celluloid images, circa 1890: Corn by Robeson, Rochester N.Y. Eagle claw by Hebbard-Spencer, Germany. Nude by Clauberg Bros., Germany. Cowboy by Clark Bros., Germany. Collection: C.W. Lyle Jr.

A patriotic trio of stars and stripes: bottle, waste bowl, and flag-decorated shaving mug. Collection: Roger Baker.

Pages 206 & 207, 1st row, left to right:
The livery stable is another stock mug having a Western feeling. Collection: Roger Baker.

California Beer and Soda is clearly painted on the side of this teamster's wagon. Collection: Roger Baker.

Blacksmiths are commonly depicted on occupational mugs, however they are not always done as nicely as this one. Collection: Roger Baker.

Pool players. Collection: Roger Baker.

2nd row, left to right:
What's black and white and read all over? It's the old limerick which gives a clue to this occupational mug. The answer is, of course, a newspaper. Collection: Roger Baker.

A wine salesman is illustrated on this piece which may be associated with the valley wine industry in northern California. Collection: Roger Baker.

This scarce Vintner or wine maker's mug was custom ordered and is an artist's impression of the owner at work. Collection: Roger Baker.

The Kohn Barber Supply Company produced this mug for a harness or saddle maker. Collection: Roger Baker.

3rd row, left to right:
A farrier is depicted here. Collection: Roger Baker.

Colt single-action revolvers are depicted on this mug which also features a Masonic symbol. It would enhance both a fraternal or occupational (gunsmith) collection. Collection: Roger Baker.

Each of these mugs features Western occupations. Collection: Roger Baker.

This colorful group includes a variety of occupations. Collection: Roger Baker.

A group of occupational mugs from Western origins. Collection: Roger Baker.

William Dentzel was one of the premier carousel carvers of the 19th century. The lion with a cupid on its shoulder was Dentzel's trademark. Collection: Roger Baker.

This mug was made for a secret fraternal society whose motto "T.O.T.E." is on the Indian's headband. Collection: Roger Baker.

The bartender is one of the most common occupational mugs and this one is exceptional. Collection: Roger Baker.

4th row, left to right:

The Texas longhorn (with the knife and steel) pictured on this occupational mug is symbolic of the butcher. Collection: Roger Baker.

A grain elevator operator is illustrated on this mug. Additional decoration, including a horse drawn wagon and a train, add to its appeal and value. Collection: Roger Baker.

The Southern Pacific Railroad employed this mug's owner. It is made by Will and Finck, San Francisco, and is quite scarce. Collection: Roger Baker.

Found in the California gold country, this mug is quite rare showing a gold miner in front of the shaft. Custom painted mugs like this sometimes lack the artistic skill found on stock mugs on which artists produced the same image every day. Collection: Roger Baker.

A Texas oil man may have been the owner of this pretty mug. Collection: Roger Baker.

Chapter Sixteen

Advertising

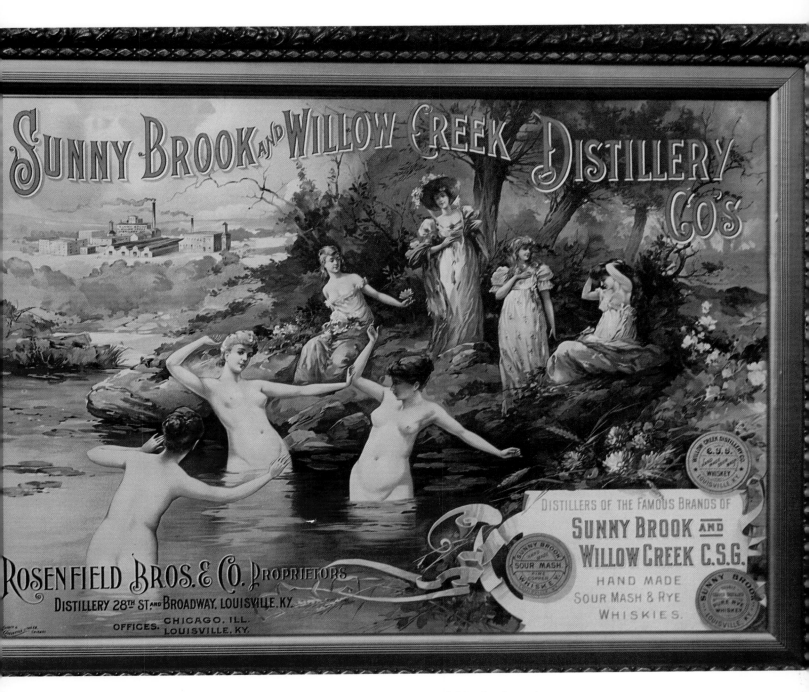

Sunny Brook was distributed in the West and this sign hung in a
Bay Area saloon, circa 1890 period, stone lithograph. Collection:
Roger Baker.

Opposite page:
Issued by Buffalo Brewing about the turn of the century, this has
long been a favorite of collectors. It was reprinted in the 1960s by
Portal Gallery. Collection: Roger Baker.

Yosemite is a famous old beer sign from California. It has wonderful color and is in excellent condition. Collection: Roger Baker.

The California Bear reverse glass sign is one of the most sought after Western signs, circa 1900 to 1905. Collection: Roger Baker.

Olympia Beer sign made by the Dows Company (1900-1905). Olympia had distributors throughout the West, including San Francisco. Collection: Roger Baker.

Schlitz sign with glue chip letters, circa 1905. Collection: Roger Baker.

Advertisement for White Star Rye. The Cowboy and the city slicker toasting each other and beautiful graphics make this late nineteenth century piece very desirable. Collection: Allan Katz.

Reverse glass signs are painted from the back using some very exacting and labor-intensive procedures. This one encompasses some of the most demanding, including inlaid mother-of-pearl in each of the windows of the Distillery. Jas. E. Pepper had distribution throughout the West. Scarce. Collection: Roger Baker.

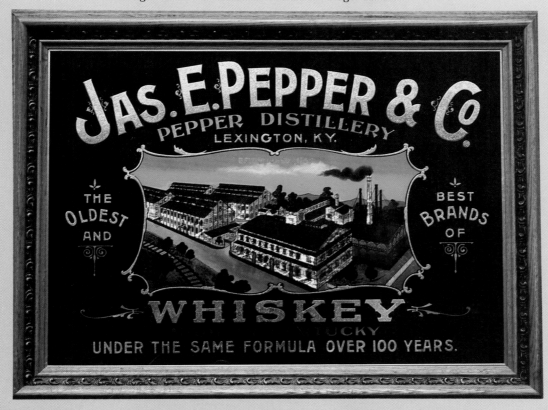

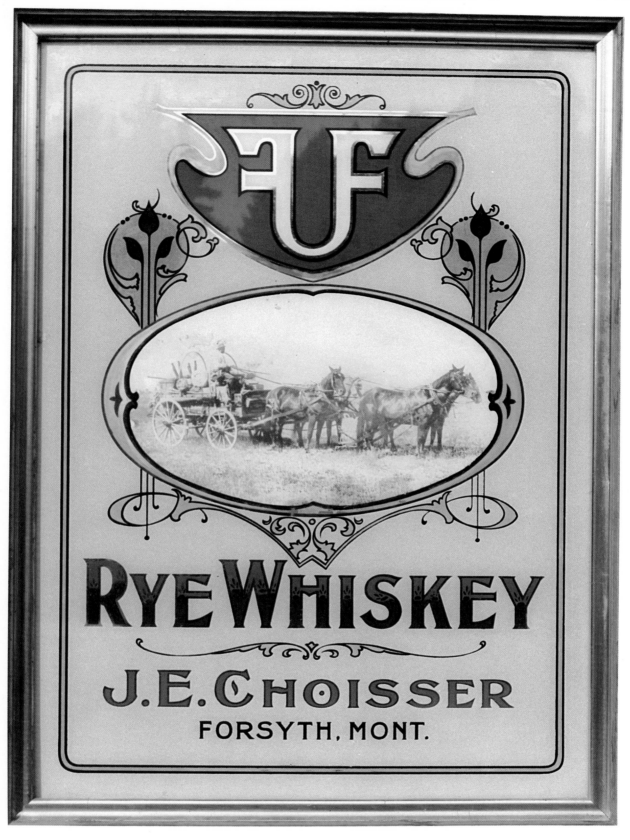

The FUF logo featured on this sign represents the brand used by this horse ranch, owned by J.E. Choisser in Montana. Famous Western photographer L.A. Huffman provided the photography. There are two images known: this one, and a second one having riders on horseback. Careful examination discloses the FUF brand on the horses pictured. Most collectors view this as one of the great Western advertising pieces, circa early-1890s. Note the Art Nouveau design. Collection: Roger Baker.

Opposite page:
Bitters was a popular alcoholic beverage in the 1800s. Produced in Chicago for the San Francisco market, the bottle label includes the city address. This is an early 1890s chromolithograph. Collection: Roger Baker.

We were following up the U.P. Railroad and the emigrant trains were full of people going West, so we thought we would give them a thrill. One day we made a dummy man suffed with grass, put a rope around his neck, and threw the other end over the crossbar of a telegraph pole. Just as the train pulled in, I yanked him up by the rope around my saddle horn, and the whole outfit began to shoot at him as he swung in the air. They shot the rope in two and down he came; someone handed me the rope, and away I went on a dead run across the flat, dragging him, the whole outfit right after me, shooting, as he bounced along. The people on the train were scared to death. Women fainted and children screamed. They begged the conductor to pull out before we held up the train. Somebody even telegraphed Lincoln saying the FUF cowboys had hung a horse thief.

We Pointed Them North

Advertisement for E.I. DuPont de Nemours & Co. Gunpowder. Late nineteenth century. Collection: Allan Katz.

Early San Francico gold rush period advertising, copyrighted in 1862. This is a hand-colored Currier and Ives lithograph advertising Gold Rush supplies as well as early firearms like Henry rifles, Colts and Sharps. The artist, A.F. Tait, was well known in the 1800s. Most early San Francisco advertising was destroyed by the earthquake and fire of 1906. Collection: Roger Baker.

Advertising graphics depicting Western themes were quite popular. Those which date prior to 1900 are especially desirable. This Mexican cowboy chased by Indians incorporates humor and reality on this 1898, U.M.C. calendar. Collection: Roger Baker.

Buffalo calendar by the Union Metallic Cartridge Co. This is a chromolithograph, as are most of the pre-1915 printed posters. Collection: Roger Baker.

The art for this Winchester calendar was painted by W.R. Leigh and is one of the few commercial pieces done by him for any company. It has all of the elements of drama that charactize his work, and ranks him among the best of Western artists. Collection: Roger Baker.

The Winchester Arms Company produced some wonderful posters and artist Lyn Bogue Hunt was responsible for many of them including this piece. The firearms companies in the early 1900s hired some of the best artists of the period. Collection: Roger Baker.

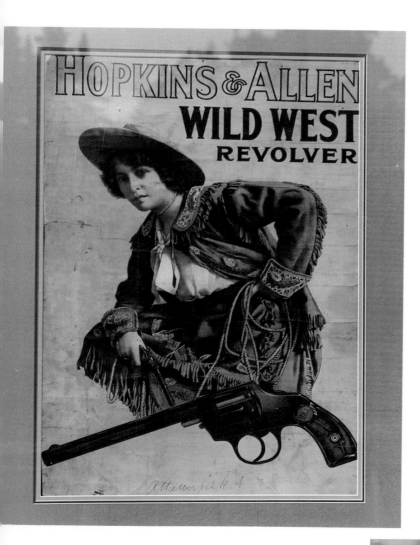

This Wild West revolver with the Hopkins & Allen girl dressed in her buckskins is about as Western as a poster can be. It is scarce in any condition. Collection: Roger Baker.

The "Cowboys and Indians" story is vividly portrayed in this 1920s period Smith & Wesson poster. Strong color and action to make this piece special. Caution: this piece has been reproduced. Collection: Roger Baker.

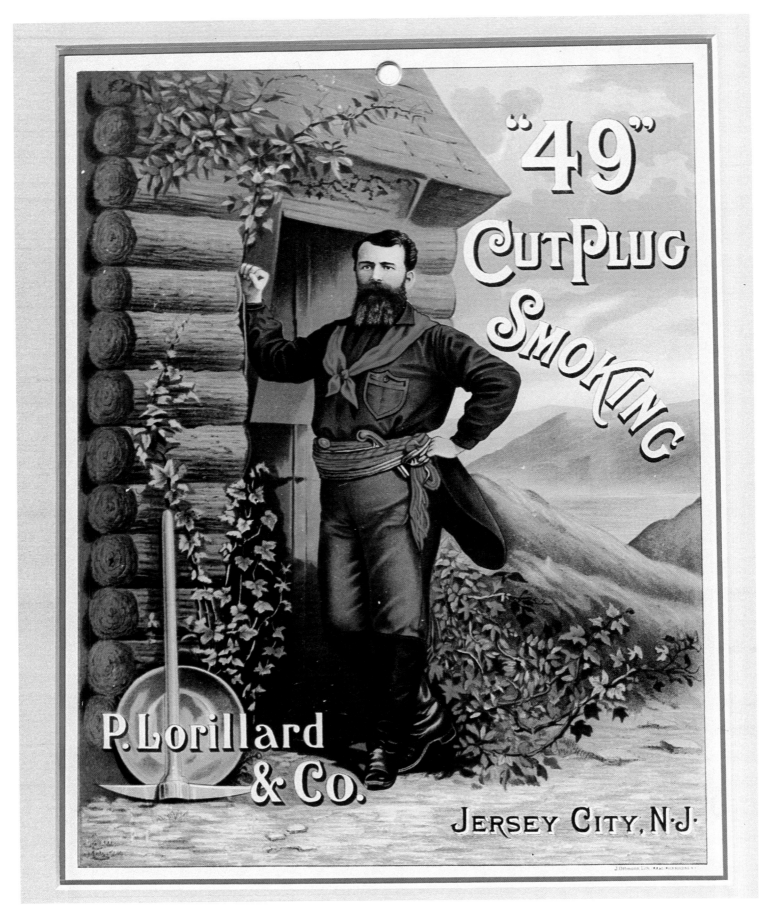

It would be difficult to find an advertising piece with a stronger connection to the California Gold Rush than this Tobacco advertising sign. The pick, gold, high-top boots, and early pepper-box pistol are all accouterments of the '49er. Chromolithograph probably dating from the late-19th century. Collection: Roger Baker.

This John Ruskin Cigars sign is one of the most dramatic cowboy
images to appear in any advertising. Collection: Roger Baker.

Advertising change trays like this one for Yokuai Bros. Cigars were common to every saloon cigar counter but are now hard to find. They are usually glass with labels underneath, circa 1880 to 1910. Collection: Roger Baker.

Tobacco pouch with Buffalo Bill style cowboy on label. Also included were cards for collecting which showed various cowboy scenes. These were promotional pieces for Hassan Cigarettes, circa 1903. Collection: Vic Williams.

Advertising change tray, circa 1898. Collection: Vic Williams.

Cigar cutter featuring a small reverse glass front panel and two cutters for different sized cigars. It dates from about 1900 and is a standard model found with different cigar makers' names. Collection: Roger Baker.

Havana cigars art plate. These plates were used at the turn of the century as promotional items. Collection: Roger Baker.

Tobacco tin circa 1890-1910, Dixie Queen brand. Desirable image and condition. Collection: Jame Mackie.

The Celestino cigar cutter has an unusual feature: depressing the cutter lever causes the round disc advertising panel to rotate 180 degrees. Original cranberry shade, circa 1875 to 1895. Collection: Roger Baker.

Cigar cutter. Silver overlay on ivory, mellow patina. Collection: C.W. Lyle, Jr.

Cigar lighters were made with and without advertising. The Y.B. pictured here is an especially fine example, with an original marked shade and cast iron marquee. This piece is scarce and dates from 1875 to 1890. Collection: Roger Baker.

Chapter Seventeen

Gambling

Gambling was nearly an obsession in the Old West. It was the common denominator among all men, and the predominant source of recreation. Everyone gambled, even the Indians. Professional gamblers appeared in great numbers in California as early as 1850 to attempt to liberate some of the good fortune realized in the gold rush. San Francisco had gambling houses of every size, among them The Alhambra, The El Dorado, Bella Union and The Empire. In a gala atmosphere complete with whiskey, women and music, the oft-times naive and unsophisticated miners, cowboys and loggers lay prey to the slick and often unscrupulous gambler. Most gamblers made their money a little at a time, since there were few high rollers and the average cowboy or miner had little money to gamble. So popular was gambling that a small industry sprang up just for the manufacture of cheating devices.

The most popular game of chance was faro followed by roulette, black jack, and sometime later, craps. Bets were made in gold and silver coins as well as paper currency which was issued by local banks, but as often as not, gold dust itself was wagered by the ounce. Dishonest miners would supplement the gold with brass shavings, but by and large, the gamblers always had an enormous advantage. Gambling was not limited to the Gold Rush era, for throughout the last half of the 19th century, local townspeople, railroad workers and just about everybody else was known to partake in their favorite game of chance. Although women gamblers were a rare sight, there were

Tools of the trade for a 19th century gambler in the Old West. Collection: Thomas W. Connally.

Individual place card holders with a playing card motif, circa 1910 to 1930. Collection: C.W. Lyle, Jr.

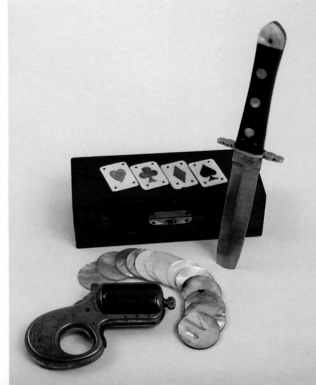

Dice drops, a countertop game, circa 1920s, made by H.C. Evans, Chicago. Collection: Vic Williams.

Miniature chuck-a-luck, circa pre-Civil War, made with hand blown glass and hand forged metal parts. Collection: Vic Williams.

Large ivory dice with hand engraved or scrimshawed letters which seem to spell CRAPES. Collection: Roger Baker.

some notable exceptions such as "Poker Alice" Ivers and Belle Siddons. Old photographs of cowboys show scenes of card games in the bunkhouse and out on the range. Gambling was not just confined to saloons, in fact Westerners would gamble on almost anything including foot races, horse races, and cock fights.

The flavor of the Old West can be experienced through the gambler's tools of trade. These rare antiques form an image of frontier life with all it's bawdy allure. Especially intriguing are the cheating devices since they tell of a far more risky and provacative game. Gamblers went to great lengths to gain the edge and at great peril to life and limb.

The best known manufacturer of saloon and gambling accoutrements was the San Francisco firm of Will and Finck which made everything from lemon squeezers to nail pricks (used for marking cards). Gamblers could order by mail anything needed for an honest or dishonest game of chance. For example, Will and Finck offered nineteen different kinds of dealing boxes, of which only three were honest. Items made by Will and Finck are of fine quality and are very desirable.

Keno Goose, circa early-1900s. The hopper contained a concealed cheating device. Collection: Vic Williams.

Keno Goose, circa 1920s, made by H.G. Evans & Co., Chicago. Collection: Vic Williams.

Mechanical dice shaker, with an ivory dice cup and bone dice, circa late 1800s. Collection: Vic Williams.

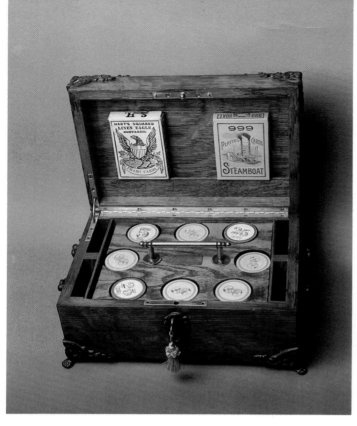

The El Dorado Saloon was founded at the dawn of the Gold Rush in 1849, and was home for this set of ivory chips. Each chip is marked with a stylized logo "ELDO" in addition to the numerical value. Marked Will & Finck. Collection: Roger Baker.

Opposite page:
Beautiful dyed mother-of-pearl poker chips with hand scrimshawed designs are both fine and rare. Collection: C.W. Lyle, Jr.

Rare French set of mother-of-pearl gambling chips, circa late-1800s, in a box marked "H. Pussey, 20 Rue De La Bargue." Collection: Vic Williams.

Beautiful and rare cased set of mother-of-pearl poker chips in red, yellow, blue and white, circa 1890. Collection: C.W. Lyle, Jr.

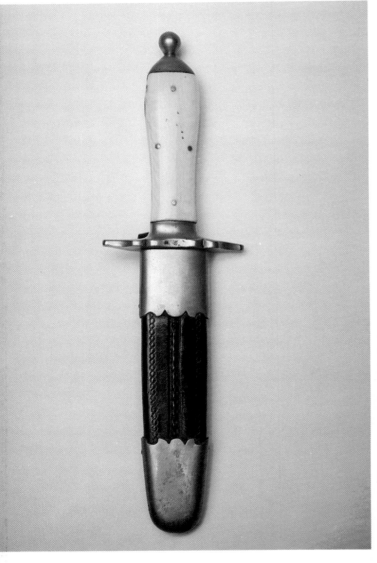

19th century bone handled gentleman's knife with original sheath. Collection: C.W. Lyle, Jr.

Two examples of poker "bucks," circa 1890, which were used to denote the position of the last dealer. The term "the buck stops here" originated from the use of poker bucks or deal markers. Collection: C.W. Lyle, Jr.

A deck of round-up playing cards, circa 1900, featuring a mounted vaquero on the back and a cloth-bound carrying case together with an ivory-gripped, fully-engraved, .32 caliber "hide-out" gun, circa 1860s. The front of the carrying case reads "A history of a King & Queen" while the spine reads "Let us play." The joker has been substituted for the six of spades cover. Collection: Douglas Deihl.

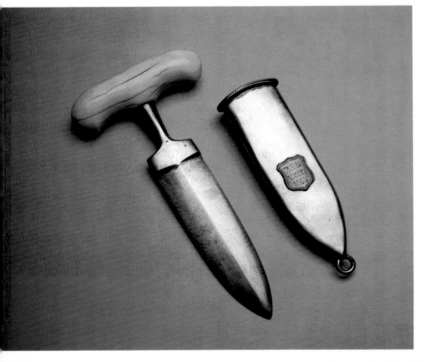

Gambler's dirk or push dagger with an ivory handle marked "Will & Finck—S.F. Cal." The sheath for the dagger has an internal, spring-like device to hold the dagger in place so it could not "fall" out. This dirk came from the famous mining town of Virginia City, Neveda. Collection: Dr. James Brown.

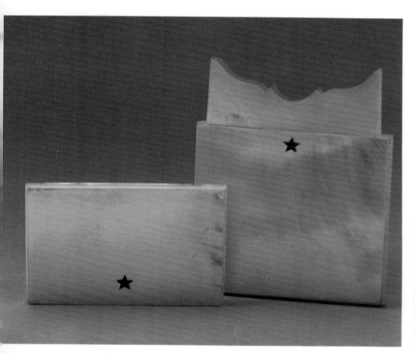

Handmade mother-of-pearl card case with inlaid stars, possibly belonged to a gambler. Collection: Michael Friedman.

Fancy, cut-velvet, double breasted gambler's vest, circa late-1870s to 1880's. Collection: Vic Williams.

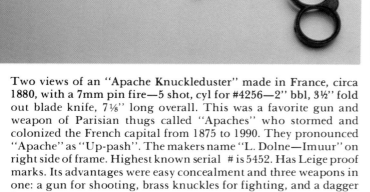

Two views of an "Apache Knuckleduster" made in France, circa 1880, with a 7mm pin fire—5 shot, cyl for #4256—2" bbl, 3½" fold out blade knife, 7⅛" long overall. This was a favorite gun and weapon of Parisian thugs called "Apaches" who stormed and colonized the French capital from 1875 to 1990. They pronounced "Apache" as "Up-pash". The makers name "L. Dolne—Imuur" on right side of frame. Highest known serial # is 5452. Has Leige proof marks. Its advantages were easy concealment and three weapons in one: a gun for shooting, brass knuckles for fighting, and a dagger for close work. Collection: Dr. James Brown.

Early cufflinks containing three ivory dice under a domed glass. The dice shake freely and can be used for gambling, circa 1880. Collection: C.W. Lyle, Jr.

Heads or Tails? Sterling silver flipping coins. One features an
elephant front and back, one a donkey, and the third, a horse.
Collection: C.W. Lyle, Jr.

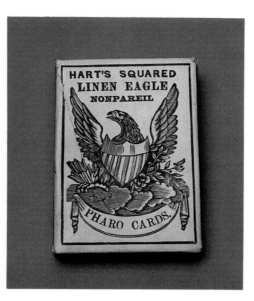

Samuel Hart faro cards were the standard in saloons of the Old West. These have an 1863 patent date. Collection: Roger Baker.

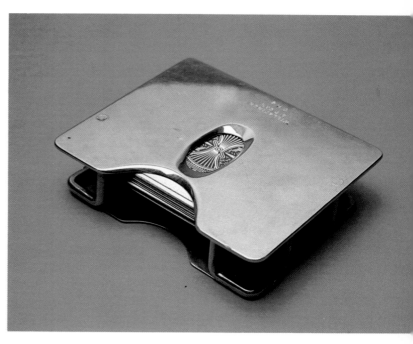

A skeleton style dealing box by Will & Finck of San Francisco, which was used in the games of faro and black- and-red. Collection: Roger Baker.

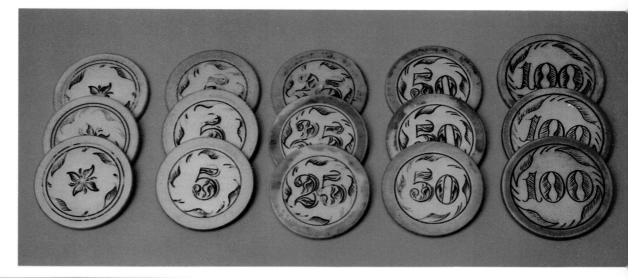

A Scrimshaw ivory poker chips, circa 1860s. The $50 and $100 denominations are are. Collection: Vic Williams.

This boxed set of brass poker clips was an advertising piece for Brown Brothers Cigars. It is said to be similar to a set used by Wyatt Earp in Tombstone, Arizona in the late 1800s. Collection: Roger Baker.

This Victorian assemblage of gaming-related paraphernalia includes ivory dominoes, a jack-pot marker, ivory put- and-take dice, a silver put-and-take, enamelled cuff links, 2 enamelled match safes (one with cards and the other with a nude slave scene) and a silver and gold money clip. Collection: Roger Baker.

Brass game counter with a (pointer) dog motif as the pointer. Collection: C.W. Lyle, Jr.

Game counter made of ivory and rosewood. Collection: C.W. Lyle, Jr.

An elaborate, embossed and engraved game counter to prevent cheating with a bell that rings when the pointer is moved. Collection: C.W. Lyle, Jr.

Everness advertising token which could be filled with liquid and squirted out as a joke. Collection: C.W. Lyle, Jr.

Gambler's silver matchsafe decorated with a hand holding five cards superimposed over coins. Collection: C.W. Lyle, Jr.

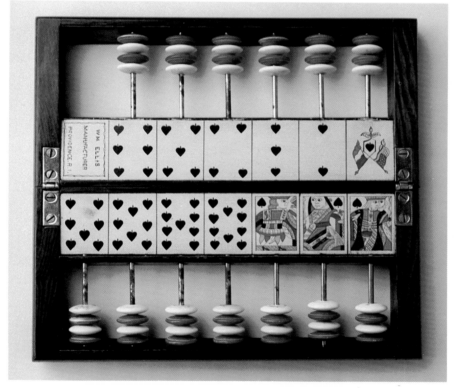

This 19th century casekeeper kept track of the number and rank of cards played. Collection: Roger Baker.

This large, sterling silver put-and-take by Gorham Silver Co. is one of the most sought-after. It measures approximately 2¾'' across. Collection: Roger Baker.

Token from the Gem Saloon of El Paso, Texas, circa 1890. Collection: C.W. Lyle, Jr.

Folding layout for the game of Faro. Manufactured by W.C. Evans of Chicago, IL, this board is shown in the spade suit which was most common. Collection: Roger Baker.

Set of hand scrimshawed and color filled crown and anchor dice measuring 1¼'' along each edge, circa mid 1800s. Collection: C.W. Lyle, Jr.

Cheaters

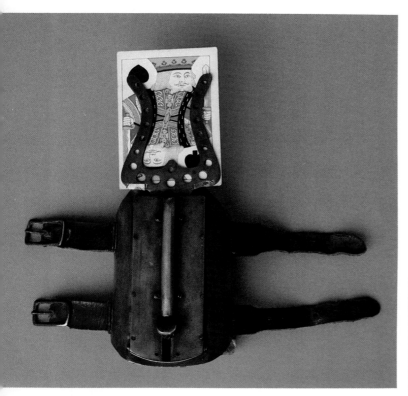

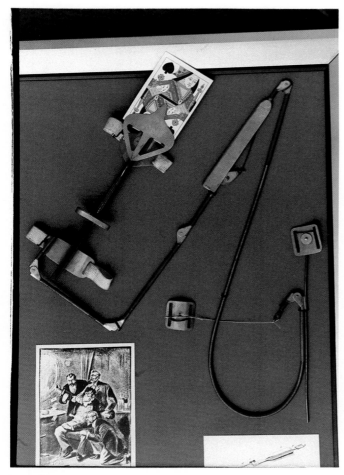

Jacob's ladder: Gambler's sleeve holdout. Hidden under his sleeve, the cheater buckled this device around his arm and at the appropriate time forced a winning card into his hand by causing the accordian-type mechanism to extend forward. Collection: William Williamson.

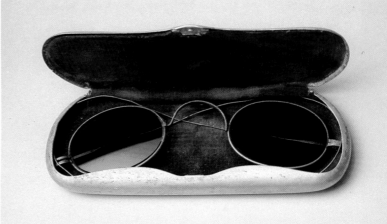

Cheating glasses with blue lenses. Cards marked with irridescent ink were visible only when wearing these glasses. Collection: C.W. Lyle, Jr.

An elaborate device for cheating at cards, devised by a man named Kepplinger. Legend has it that when this device was discovered by a group of three other professional gamblers, instead of the usual beating or hanging, Kepplinger's punishment was to make a similar device for each of the other three men. Collection: William Williamson.

Breastplate holdout. Sewn inside his coat, the unscroupulous gambler could produce an entirely new hand by means of a cord attached to his shoe or boot. He simply had to bend his leg to trigger the mechanism. Collection: William Williamson.

This innocent-looking stack of silver half-dollars contains an angled mirror enabling the dealer to peek at each card dealt, without making any suspicious moves. This came from the estate of the famous Texas Ranger Frank Hamer who confiscated it in Borgher, Texas during the oil boom days. Collection: C.W. Lyle, Jr.

Card trimmers were a key part of any professional gambler's equipment. This lever-style cutter has a walrus ivory handle and adjustments for aligning cards to produce "gaffed," or crooked, decks. Collection: Roger Baker.

This bone dice top is a cheating device that allows "the man in the know" to control the outcome of each spin, circa 1890. Collection: C.W. Lyle, Jr.

Silk ''stove pipe'' top hat, circa 1860 to '70, lined in red paper with a mirror in the crown. The hat band is horse hair with silver ornament. The mirror was probably used as a cheating device by a gambler. Collection: Vic Williams.

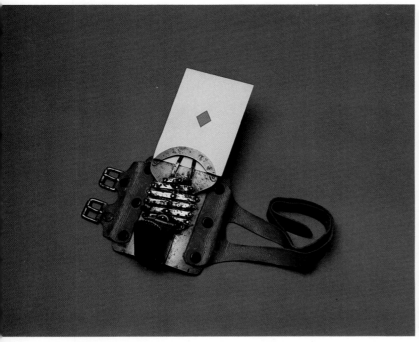

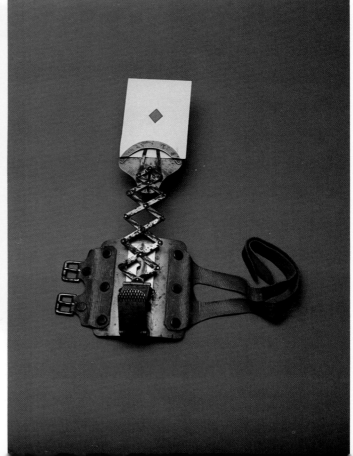

This early sleeve or arm holdout, possibly circa 1860 to 1870, was used to retreive a card up one sleeve for later use. The card would be pushed out to make a winning hand. Gamblers caught with this type of device received quick and certain frontier justice. Collection: Roger Baker.

Chapter Eighteen

Furniture

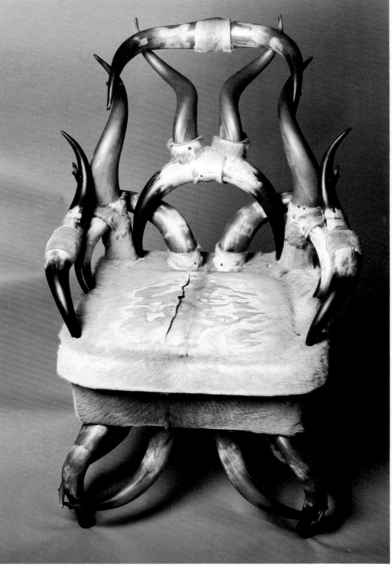

This horn chair, circa early 1900s is reported to be from the Yellow Dog Saloon in Indian territory, Guthrie, Oklahoma. Collection: Vic Williams.

An early leather and horn foot stool with date studded in a circle. Collection: C.W. Lyle, Jr.

Opposite page:
A magnificent table featuring interlaced horns with age and good color. The solid walnut top displays Plains Indian chief with headdress made in colorful parquet inlay of exceptional quality. Collection: C.W. Lyle, Jr.

This horn rocker circa 1892 is carved "made by B.F. Bery July 23, 1892, Portland, Oregon" on the bottom. Horn rocking chairs are scarce. Collection: Vic Williams.

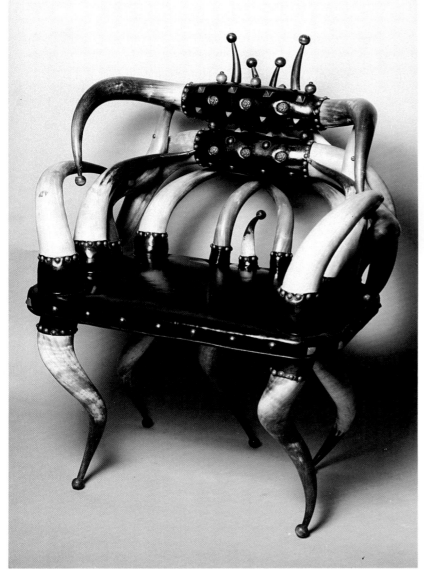

A chair made with fragile and long cattle horns of this type were often made for cattle barons as curios. Few have survived. Collection: Enrique Guerra.

Horn chair of unusual design, with Victorian velvet and fringe. Collection: Jim Holley.

Chapter Nineteen

Photography

The most accurate visual portrayal of life in the Old West is provided by photographs. As early as the California Gold Rush, photographers were recording the history of the Old West. Most towns and cities of some significance had a local photographer. Their cameras were large and cumbersome and their film was slow, but they managed to capture a most remarkable view of America in the second half of the nineteenth century. They captured the entire story, from the majestic beauty of the western landscapes to the men and women who built frontier America. These images would serve as a permanent record for posterity. Even during the period, people back East were fascinated by the stories and pictures of western life. Later, these photographs served as models for the burgeoning movie industry, dime novels and theatrical productions. When a cowboy came to town after being out on the range, it was not unusual, after having a bath and a shave, for him to have his picture taken at the local photographer's studio. Even city slickers and visiting greenhorns would dress up like cowboys and have their photos taken for the folks back home. It is through photography that we are able to learn, in great detail, about the evolution of western fashion, architecture and industry.

During the early period (1850-1860) daguerrean photography was the state of the art. This method used pure silver plated onto copper to produce images known as "Daguerreotypes." Because of the silver, daguerreotypes, or "Dags," had a mirror-like surface. After being processed, the copper plates were set in handsome book-like cases made of hard rubber. Many of these cases had beautiful designs.

Next, photography developed the Ambrotype which had a rather short history in the Old West. Unlike the copper plates of the Dags, Ambrotypes were negatives printed on glass and then painted black on the back. Their popularity lasted only until about 1865 when the Tintype became the preferred photographic method. Like it's predecessors, Tintypes were stored in hard rubber cases, but they were produced on sheets of iron which were painted black on the reverse. Finally, the paper photograph became popular in the 1860s and has been in use ever since. Small, early paper photos known as *cartes de visites* became very popular because they were much less expensive than the previous methods. Also available were cabinet cards and stereo cards which, when seen through a viewer, created a three-dimensional picture.

This rugged cowboy's face shows the effects of many years in the saddle. Collection: Ken Schatra.

A rare, turn of the century tin type photograph in a frame with no hinges and lid. The cowboy is shoeing his horse. Collection C.W. Lyle, Jr.

A tin type photograph of six 19th century cowboys. Note their hats, boots, spurs and leather chaps. Collection: C.W. Lyle, Jr.

Collecting photographs of the Old West is an especially satisfying pursuit because they tend to be priced reasonably unless signed by a well known photographer. Collectors of Old Western photos are often "image" collectors rather than traditonal photography collectors. Factors such as size and condition are important but value also depends on where a particular photo was taken, during what time frame, and who or what is depicted.

An ambrotype photograph of a gambling scene. Collection: C.W. Lyle, Jr.

A tin type photograph of a Mexican-looking cowboy with sombrero holding a Winchester model 1866. Collection: C.W. Lyle, Jr.

A period photograph of a bearded cowboy complete with hat, gun, chaps, boots and spurs, circa 1910s. Collection: C.W. Lyle, Jr.

Originally thought to be an original photograph of a gunfight, this picture was a published still for a movie called "A Debtor to the Law," which was shot in San Antonio, Texas in 1919. The scene depicts a foiled bank robbery in Stroud, Oklahoma, actually committed by Henry Starr who was related to Belle Starr. The outlaw on the ground who is shot is Henry Starr, playing himself at a time when he was actually a fugitive. Collection: Jack Ringwalt.

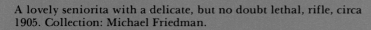

A lovely seniorita with a delicate, but no doubt lethal, rifle, circa 1905. Collection: Michael Friedman.

Interesting cross-cultural photograph depicting two Indian cowboys. It is unusual to find pictures of Indians dressed in white man's clothes, circa 1890. Collection: Michael Friedman.

"Saddling the Wild Horse" by noted western photographer, L.A. Huffman, circa 1894. Collection: Michael Friedman.

Large 11'' x 14'' portrait of a cowboy and an Indian. This rare
photograph shows two strong and proud players in the Old West.
Collection: Michael Friedman.

Cowboy at a line shack, late 19th century. Collection: Michael Friedman.

This cowpuncher is ready for action. An interesting view of a cowboy's regalia. Collection: Michael Friedman.

Collection: Michael Friedman.

Large 11'' x 14'' studio photo of a 19th century cowboy. Notice the double loop holster with a 7½'' Single Action revolver, and the fringed "shotgun" chaps. Collection: Michael Friedman.

Thus the name "Longhorns." Collection: Michael Friedman.

On October 5th, 1892, the Dalton gang attempted an audacious double bank robbery in their own hometown of Coffeyville Kansas. The ill-fated fiasco resulted in the death of four townspeople and the entire gang except for one of the brothers, Emmett Dalton who served 15 years in prison for his part. Here photographer Tackett captures the dead outlaws in their final repose. Collection: Michael Friedman.

"On the Frontier." Photo of a bunch of Bills. Notice the young "dude Billy" in center. He was probably a visitor from back East. Collection: Michael Friedman.

Large cabinet card (8" x 10") by noted photographer Grabill. "We have it rich" washing and panning gold. Rockerville Dakota. Old Timers Spriggs, lamb and Dillon at work. Grabill was based in Deadwood S. Dakota. Collection: Michael Friedman.

Advertisement for the Slaton Hotel in Georgetown, Texas, circa turn of the century. Collection: Michael Friedman.

Chapter Twenty

Wild West

WILD WEST SHOWS

William Frederick Cody, or as he was best known as Buffalo Bill was the originator of the Wild West Show. A distinctly American phenomenon, the first show was produced by Cody in his home town of North Platte Nebraska to celebrate the fourth of July in the summer of 1882. Buffalo Bill was at this time already a famous scout and had spent ten years doing stage melodrama. Billed as North Platte's "Old Glory Blow Out", this event not only marked the beginning of the Wild West Show, but also probably the Rodeo as we know it. In the beginning, the concept was more a competition in roping, shooting, riding, and bronco breaking, but it later evolved into an incredible production of entertainment relating to the wild west including re-enacted battles between cowboys and real indians (mostly sioux), trick shooting from the likes of Annie Oakley and acrobatics much like those one might see in a circus. In a sense, the Wild West show was a bridge between the early cowboy period and the Hollywood cowboy era. It kept alive both the legend of the American Cowboy and the spirit of the Old West in the first quarter of the nineteenth century. The idea was an enormous success and Buffalo Bill's Wild West show became a hit throughout America and Europe. As Cody's fame spread, more than a hundred different shows would follow, some of which were quite successful. One of the biggest was the Miller Brothers 101 Ranch Wild West show. With stars such as Tom Mix, Stack Lee and Bill Pickett, the 101 Wild West rivalved even the great shows of Buffalo Bill.

Early photograph of Buffalo Bill on a celluloid button with an easel back, circa 1910. Collection: C.W. Lyle, Jr.

Child's Buffalo Bill book with beautiful lithographic images depicting the adventures (both real and imagined) of Buffalo Bill Cody, circa 1887. Collection: Michael Friedman.

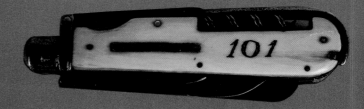

Turn of the century cowboy knife with unusual horseshoe cleaning blade. Bone handle inscribed 101 and Ponca City reveal that this knife was no doubt carried by a cowboy with the 101 Ranch Wild West Show. Collection: Ruth and Jerry Murphey.

A souvenir Program of "The new 101 Ranch Real Wild West and Great Far East Show. 1927 issue." The shows for 1924 to 1927 sometimes used the same cover stories and pictures. The feature story is of the Cherokee Strip Cow Punchers' Association organized by Joe Miller in 1920 for all cowhands who worked the Cherokee Strip prior to the opening of the land for settlement in 1893. The Association met annually on the ranch until 1958. Collection: Jerry and Ruth Murphey.

Inside double spread image from the Buffalo Bill Child's book. Circa 1887. Collection: Michael Friedman.

Poster by The Strobridge Lithograph Co. of Cincinnati & New York, 29'' x 39'' lithograph, circa 1914, which features Zack T., Joe C. and George L. Miller leading the parade of performers. Collection: Jerry and Ruth Murphey.

"Bury Me not on the Lone Prairie" was another great song for awhile, but it ended up just like a lot of songs on the radio today; they sung it to death. It was a saying on the range that even the horses nickered it and the coyotes howled it; it got so they'd throw you in the creek if you sang it. I first heard it along about '81 or '82, and by '85 it was prohibited.

We Pointed Them North

MILLER BROS. &
ARLINGTON

101
RANCH
REAL
WILD WEST

MAGAZINE AND DAILY REVIEW
PRICE 10 CENTS

Catlinite Indian Peace Pipe with the bowl carved with the 101 Ranch logo and inscribed "Joe C. Miller". Joe, "Joe Coga" (Friend Joe), was presented with a peace pipe when he was elected Chief of the Ponca Indian Tribe. Little Standing Buffalo, sub-chief under Chief White Eagle, asked that when he died, Joe C. Miller would take his place. This is an honor given to few white men. Collection: Jerry and Ruth Murphey.

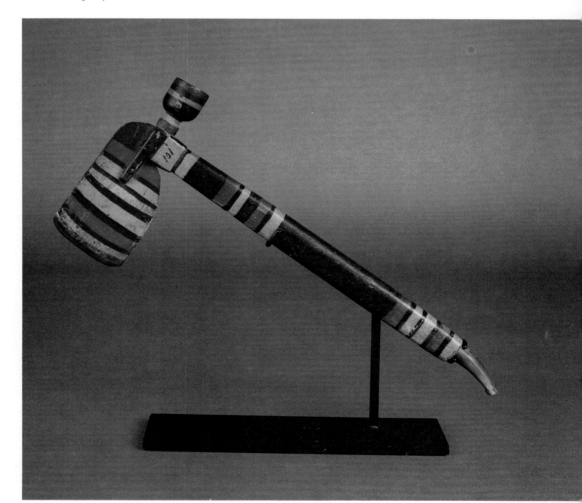

Opposite page:
Magazine and Daily Review front cover lithograph from the Strobridge Ltho. Co., copyright 1911, circa 1915. The program of events and performers are listed. The centerfold picture is Jess Willard's knockout of Jack Johnson when he won the Heavyweight Championship of the World on April 5, 1915. Collection: Jerry and Ruth Murphey.

Painted peace pipe, tomahawk made by the Ponca Indians and used in the 101 Wild West Show, circa 1910. Collection: Michael Friedman.

Postcard photograph of Stack Lee, circa 1920s. Lee was an all-around cowboy and one of the world's top trick shot artists. He was with the 101 Ranch Wild West Show in London in 1914 and still with them when the show went broke in Washington D.C. in 1931. Collection: Jerry and Ruth Murphey.

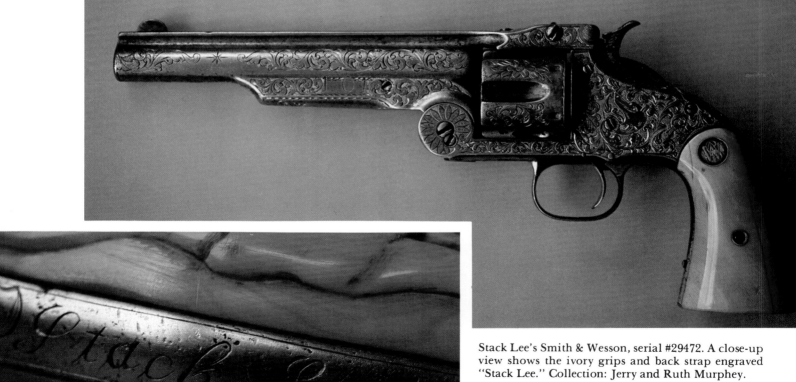

Stack Lee's Smith & Wesson, serial #29472. A close-up view shows the ivory grips and back strap engraved "Stack Lee." Collection: Jerry and Ruth Murphey.

"TEXAS" COOPER
WITH "THE ROUND UP"

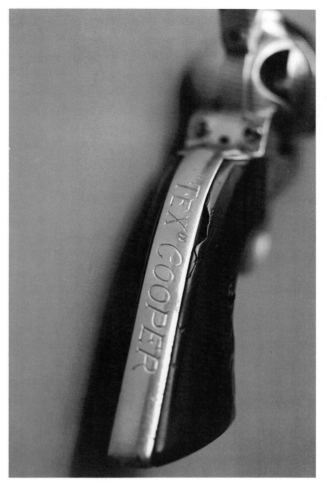

A picture post card of "Texas" Cooper, published by the Rose Company, Phila. Pa., circa 1900. "Texas" or "Tex" Cooper was a trick shot artist, mail agent, and arena director for the 101 Ranch Wild West show for many years. In 1925 he was Deputy United States Marshal in charge of Indians. He was also with Buffalo Bill and Pawnee Bill's Wild West Shows and made movies on the 101 Ranch and in California as early as 1910. He continued to have bit parts until he died in 1951. Collection: Jerry and Ruth Murphey.

Close up of "Tex Cooper" engraved on back strap of his gun. Collection: Jerry and Ruth Murphey.

Poster pictured in a 1913 program which shows Theodore Roosevelt congratulating "Goldie St. Clair, Girl Bucking Horse Rider. Theodore Roosevelt visited the 101 Ranch and the Wild West Show. Collection: Jerry and Ruth Murphey.

An offical review program with color lithograph cover published by I.M. Southern & CO., New York and Cincinnati, Ohio, circa 1910. It lists events and stories about the 101 Ranch. Collection: Jerry & Ruth Murphey.

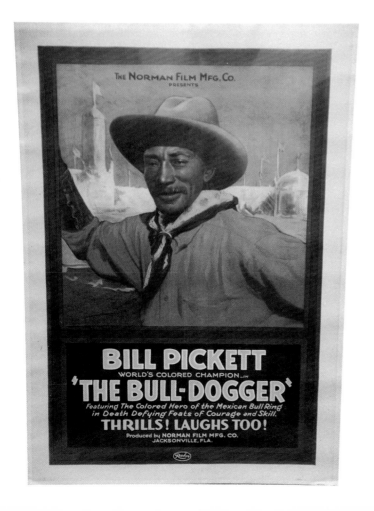

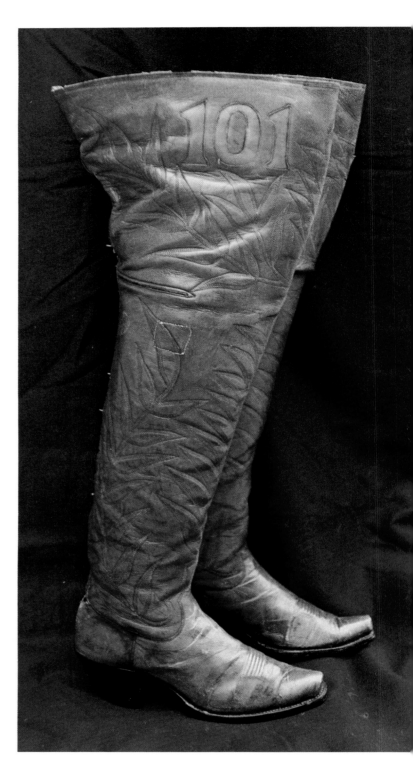

Zack T. Miller's above-the-knee show boots. Made of Kangaroo skin. Pictures show him wearing boots in the 1920s and 1930s. Collection: Jerry & Ruth Murphey.

A silent-era movie poster of Bill Pickett, circa 1913, 27'' x 41'', a real cowboy who appeared with the Miller Bros.' 101 Ranch Wilkd West Show from 1905 to 1931. Bill Pickett was the originator of Rodeo Bulldogging. He died on the ranch in 1932. This silent film was exclusively about Bill Pickett and his bulldogging of a Mexican fighting bull in Mexico City in 1912. Collection: Jerry & Ruth Murphey.

Belt Buckles

Buckle A: Made by Maddox Western, Amarillo, Texas, this marked sterling and 10K trophy buckle is from the Black Hills Round Up of 1955 for the winner of the calf roping contest.

Buckle B: A sterling buckle with 10K steerhead which is unmarked, but the engraving is in the best Bohlin style, circa 1930s to 1940s.

Buckle C: Buckle by Sunset Trails marked sterling and 10K, circa 1940s to 1950s. Sunset Trails was a prominent maker in the Southern California area which still makes buckles today.

Buckle D: Buckle from "La Grange Rodeo, 1959" made by Ray La Tourneau, a California maker.

Buckle E: An unmarked sterling and 14K buckle commemorating the "Shoshone Indian Pow Wow" in the Pacific Northwest, circa 1950s.

Buckle F: A buckle by the Diablo Manufacturing Company marked Sterling and Jewelers Bronze, given to the champion bull rider at the Boneli Ranch Rodeo in Saugus, 1944.

Buckle G: Buckle by the Diablo Manufacturing Company marked Silver and Jewelers Bronze, given to the champion bull rider at the Tulare Rodeo in 1945.

All buckles collection: High Noon.

New Mexico High School Rodeo buckle from Santa Rosa, N. M., circa 1973, made by Diablo with sterling silver, engraved silver beads, and a gold bull and rider. Collection: High Noon.

This sterling and 14K gold trophy buckle was won at the 1942 Hoot Gibson Rodeo in San Francisco by champion Eddie Rogers. It bears no maker's mark. Collection: High Noon.

A belt buckle made from a Texas lawman's badge which belonged to C.E. Pinkerton of Harris County, Houston, Texas, early 20th century. Collection: Enrique Guerra.

Sterling silver buckle set with rubies from the 1940s. Collection: High Noon.

Engraved sterling and 10K gold trophy buckle with four rubies, 1953, awarded by Levi Strauss for the Girl's Rodeo Association's Champion Calf Roper. Made by the Nelson Company. Collection: High Noon.

Sterling and gold trophy buckle for a Shoshone Indian Pow Wow from the Pacific North West, circa 1960. It has gold nuggets, a 1910 ten dollar gold coin, and a gold peace pipe. Collection: High Noon.

A ¾'' buckle set by Edward H. Bohlin with sterling silver, gold scroll overlay, and rope edge, circa 1940s. Collection: High Noon.

A ⅝'' buckle and four-piece sterling and 10K Ranger set. Hand made and set with 5 rubies by Driskell, Rosenburg, Texas. It is marked with the name "Swipes," circa 1930s to 1940s. Collection: High Noon.

Made by Edward H. Bohlin, this ¾'' silver and gold ranger buckle has rubies, circa 1930s to 1940s. Collection: High Noon.

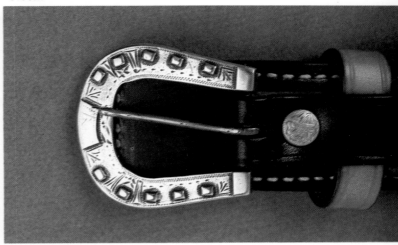

An unmarked silver and 10K pink gold ¾'' belt buckle, circa 1940s. Collection: High Noon.

A miniature three-piece ranger set made for a watch band which is marked "Hand made," Holt, Fresno (California) with a gold horsehead, four rubies and eight diamonds, circa 1930s. Collection: High Noon.

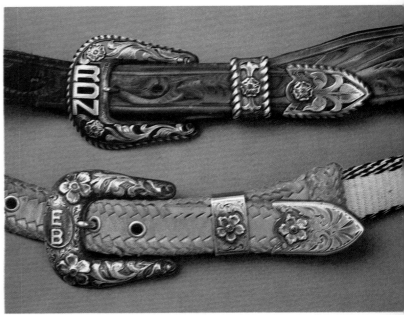

Top: Filagree buckle set by Edward H. Bohlin, No. 355 made with silver and three-color gold overlay and four rubies. The point of the buckle tongue is also gold mounted. This buckle set belonged to rodeo champion Don Nesbitt and bears his initials, circa 1930s. Nesbitt was the World Champion Cowboy in 1932.

Bottom: Bohlin-made buckle set No. 158 with silver base and beautifully engraved gold scroll overlay. Flowers, set with rubies, and a shield are also gold, circa 1940s. Collection: High Noon.

Chapter Twentytwo

Cap Guns

When the manufacturers of cowboy cap guns retired a model or went out of business, they had no idea that the toys would one day be collectable or valuable. The dies were either lost or destroyed and very few records remain. We can only guess how many cap guns were produced and while it was certainly hundreds of thousands, it is surprising how few have survived in good condition. Many of us have an indelible mental picture of our favorites, and we can never forget the way they looked, the way they felt, and without question, the way they smelled. There are few smell memories as strong as the mixture of oil, gunpowder and burned paper.

The cowboy cap guns of the 1930s, '40s and '50s were an outgrowth of the Hollywood cowboy. They often carried the name or signature of a particular movie star such as Roy Rogers, Gene Autry, The Lone Ranger, or Hopalong Cassidy. But also popular were those with names like Texan, Stallion, '49er or Fanner. When the television cowboys appeared on the scene, so did cap guns with names like Bonanza, Palladin, and Gunsmoke. But cap guns were around long before the Hollywood cowboy. Cast iron toy cap guns date back to the 1880's and were produced in many configurations. They were well made and can be as hard to find as the real guns they were made to imitate.

The cowboy cap guns of the 1930s, '40s and '50s were generally intended to resemble the Colt Peacemaker to one degree or another. Some makers such as Nichols, Kilgore, Stevens and Hubley (to name a few) did a remarkable job. It would be hard to imagine a manufacturer today producing a toy of this quality as the cost alone would make it prohibitive.

Texas Jack. Rare cast iron cap pistol, circa 1886, maker: Ives. Collection: Vic Williams.

Lion, rare, circa 1887. Maker: Ives. Collection Vic Williams.

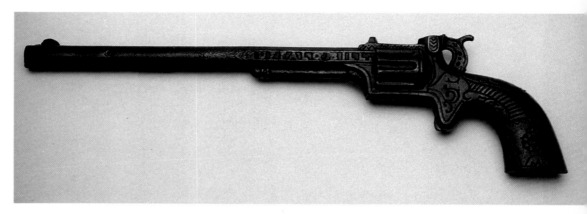

Buffalo Bill. Cast iron cap pistol, circa 1890. Maker: Stevens. Collection: Vic Williams.

Sambo, scarce, circa 1887. Maker: Ives. Collection: Vic Williams.

Animated cast iron *Monkey with coconut*, circa 1878. Maker: Stevens Mfg. The monkey cracks the coconut down on a rock which holds the cap. Collection: Vic Williams.

Crack. Very rare, double-barrel, cast iron cap pistol, circa pre-1900. Maker: Ives. Collection: Vic Williams.

Lightning Express. Animated cast iron cap gun made by Kenton, circa 1913. The train slides forward to explode a cap at the end. Collection: Vic Williams.

Six Shot, circa 1895. Maker: Stevens Mfg. This early cast iron cap pistol has six triggers that revolve spokes in a wheel. A cap is placed between each trigger which in turn cocks and drops the hammer. Collection: Vic Williams.

Rare cast iron cap exploder. The cap is placed in the open mouth and struck by the nose of the other figure. Collection: Vic Williams.

Punch and Judy. Animated cast iron cap pistol, circa 1880. Maker: Ives. The cap is placed on Judy's back while Punch bends forward and his nose explodes the cap. Collection: Vic Williams.

Sea Serpent. Scarce, animated cast iron cap pistol, circa 1880. Maker: Stevens Mfg. The curved tail forms the pistol grip and the fin underneath is the trigger. A cap is placed in the mouth and the jaw snaps shut to fire. Collection: Vic Williams.

Cannon. Rare animated cast iron cap pistol, circa 1913, maker: Kenton Mfg. The Cannon slides forward along the barrel to explode a cap at the end. Collection: Vic Williams.

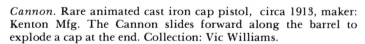

Interesting group of scarce 1930 vintage, cast iron cap guns of fine quality. Collection: Bruce Thalberg.

Cast iron cap gun circa 1915. Combination revolver and automatic styling. Internal hammer. Scarce. Manufactured by National. Collection: Bruce Thalberg.

Opposite page:
Group of circa 1920 vintage cast iron cap guns. From top, long barrel "Old Ironsides," single shot. Maker: National Mfg. *101 Ranch* long barrel, single shot named after the famous Wild West show of the same name. Maker: Kilgore Mfg. Long barrel, cast iron, single shot cap gun with the face of a man molded on grips. Maker: Kilgore Mfg. Bottom two guns are rare salesmen samples designed for display only, since there are no moving parts. Marker: Kilgore Mfg. Collection: Bruce Thalberg.

Long barrel, cast iron, roll firing cap pistol with a rare and unusually designed cap gate opening, circa 1920s. Maker: Kilgore Mfg. Collection: Bruce Thalberg.

Top: *Buffalo Bill.* Cast iron, long barrel cap gun, circa 1890. Maker: Stevens Mfg. This is in excellent condition, still retaining its original lacquer. Collection: Vic Williams.
Center: *Wild West.* Long barrel, cast iron cap gun, circa 1926. Maker: Kenton Mfg. Collection: Vic Williams.
Bottom: *Buffalo Bill,* circa 1925. Maker: Kenton Mfg. Collection Vic Williams.

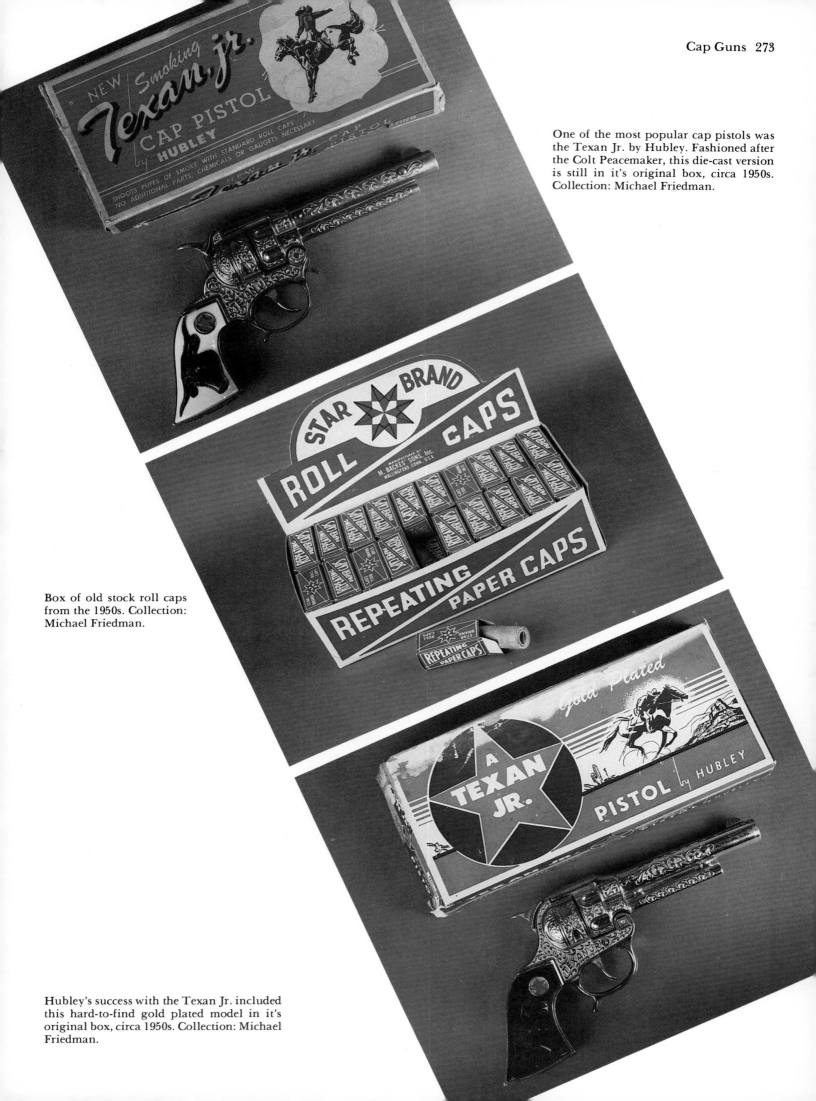

One of the most popular cap pistols was the Texan Jr. by Hubley. Fashioned after the Colt Peacemaker, this die-cast version is still in it's original box, circa 1950s. Collection: Michael Friedman.

Box of old stock roll caps from the 1950s. Collection: Michael Friedman.

Hubley's success with the Texan Jr. included this hard-to-find gold plated model in it's original box, circa 1950s. Collection: Michael Friedman.

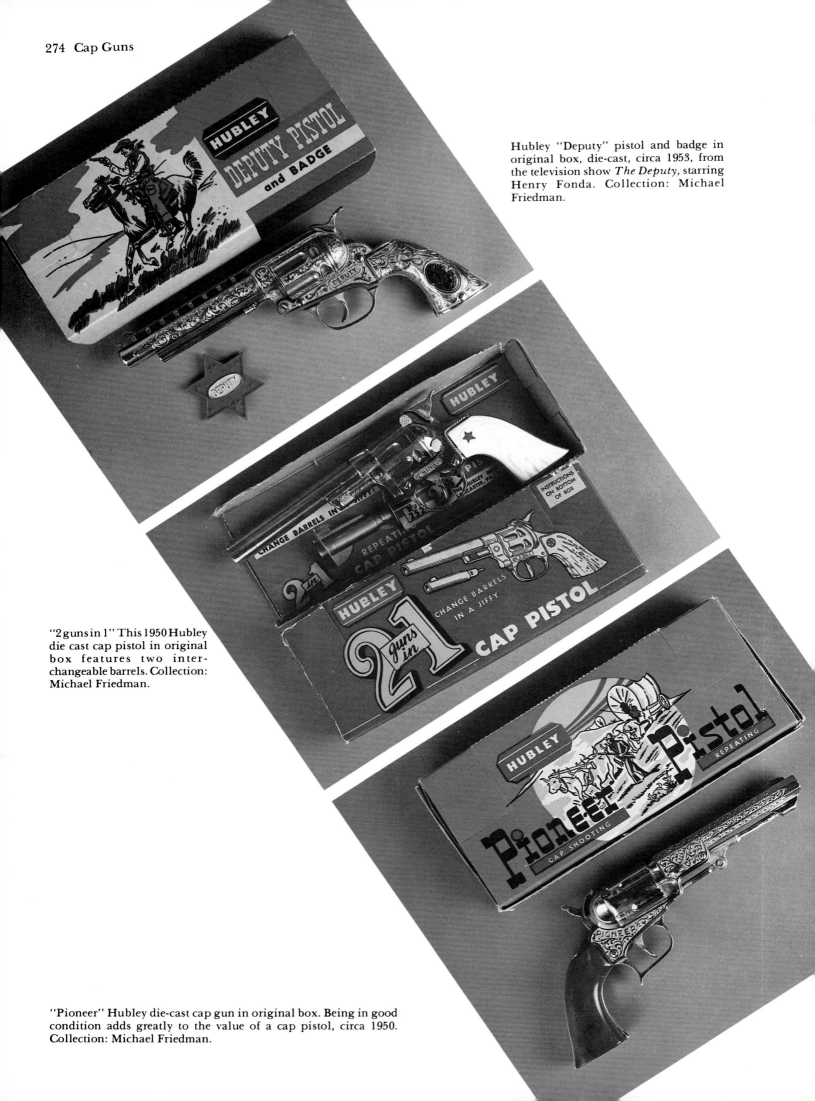

Hubley "Deputy" pistol and badge in original box, die-cast, circa 1953, from the television show *The Deputy*, starring Henry Fonda. Collection: Michael Friedman.

"2 guns in 1" This 1950 Hubley die cast cap pistol in original box features two interchangeable barrels. Collection: Michael Friedman.

"Pioneer" Hubley die-cast cap gun in original box. Being in good condition adds greatly to the value of a cap pistol, circa 1950. Collection: Michael Friedman.

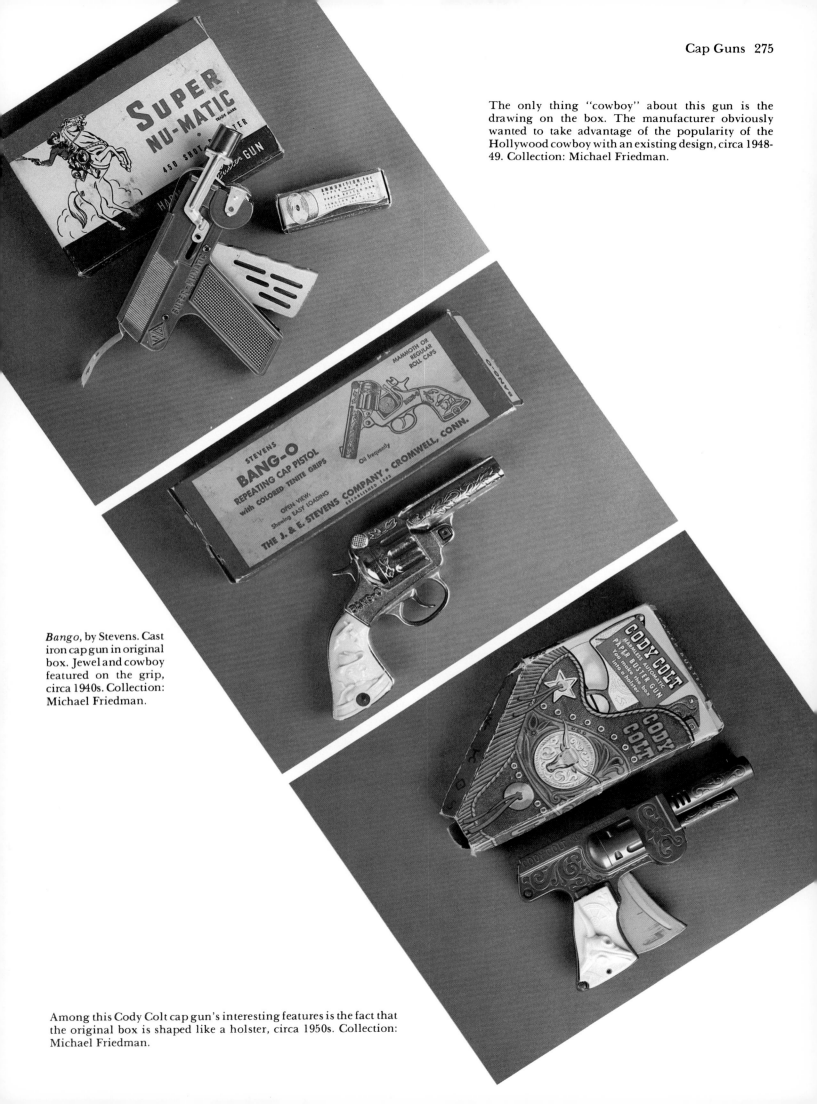

The only thing "cowboy" about this gun is the drawing on the box. The manufacturer obviously wanted to take advantage of the popularity of the Hollywood cowboy with an existing design, circa 1948-49. Collection: Michael Friedman.

Bango, by Stevens. Cast iron cap gun in original box. Jewel and cowboy featured on the grip, circa 1940s. Collection: Michael Friedman.

Among this Cody Colt cap gun's interesting features is the fact that the original box is shaped like a holster, circa 1950s. Collection: Michael Friedman.

Fine group of cast iron cap guns dating from the 1930s to 1940s. This type pre-dates the die cast variety, all are produced by Kenton Mfg. except for the two on top right which are L-H Mfg., and Wyandotte Mfg. respectively. Collection: Bruce Thalberg.

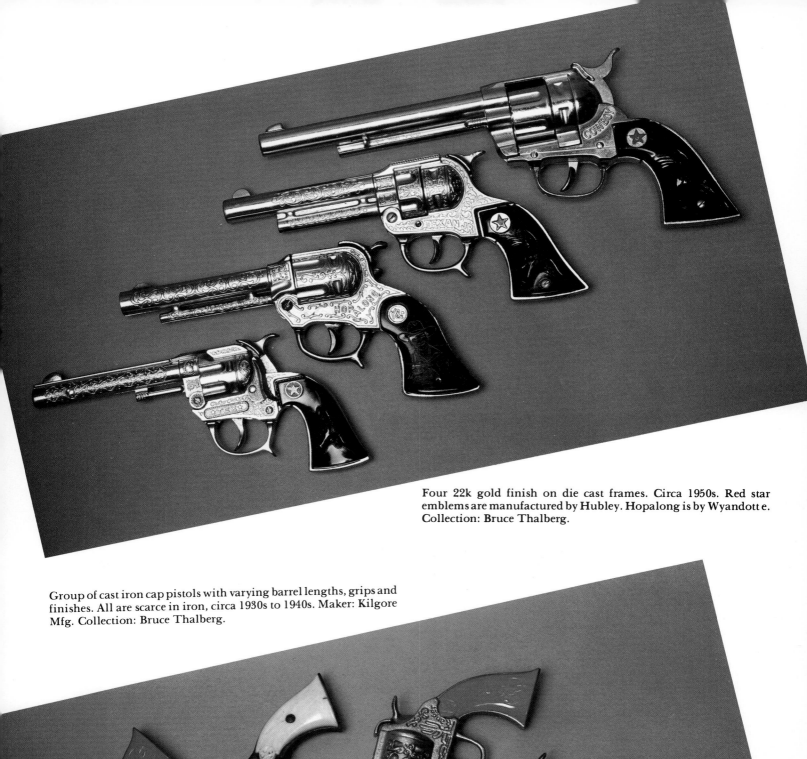

Four 22k gold finish on die cast frames. Circa 1950s. Red star emblems are manufactured by Hubley. Hopalong is by Wyandott e. Collection: Bruce Thalberg.

Group of cast iron cap pistols with varying barrel lengths, grips and finishes. All are scarce in iron, circa 1930s to 1940s. Maker: Kilgore Mfg. Collection: Bruce Thalberg.

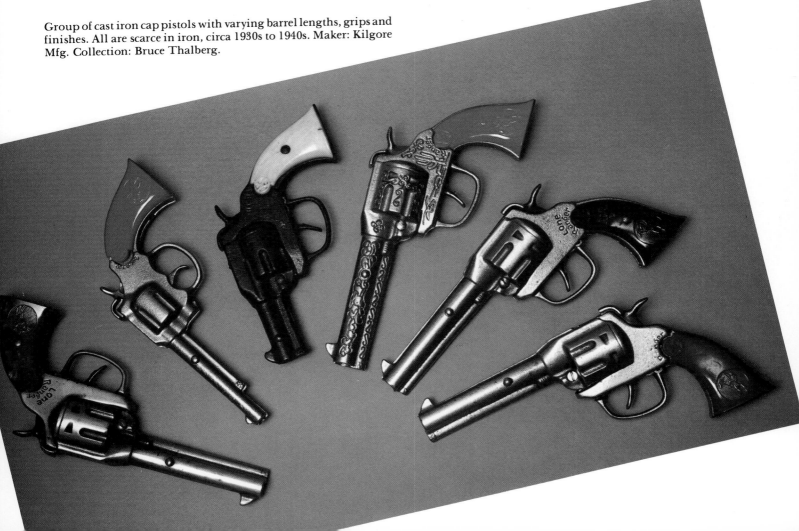

Opposite page:

Top left, clockwise:

Ranger. Cap gun of rare aluminum casting with simulated engraving and red plastic grips with horse head in relief. The single shot barrel and cylinder do not open, circa 1940s. Collection: Bruce Thalberg.

Cowpoke. Cap gun, die cast with plated finish and simulated stag grips, shoots roll caps. Note the notch bar on the grips. Shoots roll caps. Circa 1960s. Collection: Bruce Thalberg.

Cap gun with nickel finish on a cast iron frame with double action single shot, orange grips with bronco buster and simulated engraving, circa 1940s. Maker: Kenton Mfg. Collection: Bruce Thalberg.

Nickel die cast cap gun with unusual figural horse grips, circa 1950s, made by Hubley Mfg. Collection: Bruce Thalberg.

Center: Gold on iron "49er" by Stevens. Circa 1940s. Simulated ivory grips with jewel and wagon train motif. Collection: Bruce Thalberg.

This page right:

Unless closely examined, this holster could pass for the real thing. Quality such as this was rarely found with cap guns. Collection: Michael Friedman.

Bottom:

Colt 45. With a fair resemblance in appearance and size to it's name sake, this cap gun was die cast, with nickel plated frame and gold cylinder and trigger. Plain imitation ivory grips. Circa: 1950s. Maker: Hubley Mfg. This gun is special because of it's removable cylinder and because the six cartridges hold individual caps. A desirable gun for collectors. Collection: Bruce Thalberg

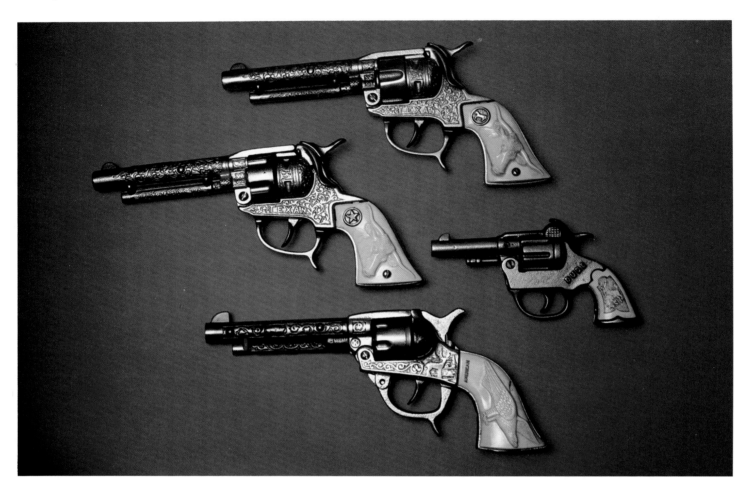

Group of four cast iron cap guns from the 1940s. These are classic Hollywood vintage guns of high quality and life-like features. They are difficult to find in this condition. Collection: Bruce Thalberg.

Die cast cap guns, circa 1950s. From top, *Roy Rogers*, with white horse grips and signature, it shoots discs or caps. Maker: Kilgore Mfg. *Buck n' Bronc* with white grips and black overlay of bronco. Maker: Geo. Schmidt. *Red Ranger*, with horseshoe and lariat grips. Maker: Wyandotte. *Kit Carson*, maker: Kilgore Mfg. Small Derringer, which fits over a stick and becomes a cane handle. Maker: Hubley.

Group of well done cast iron cap guns from the 1930s and 40s. All have imitation ivory grips and, except for *Buffalo Bill*, generic, rather than specific, names. All are in excellent condition. Collection: Bruce Thalberg.

Four die-cast plated cap guns circa early 50's. Small scale for smaller hands. all have imitation engraving. Collection: Bruce Thalberg.

Group of T.V. cowboy hero cap guns. From top: *Maverick, The Deputy, Roy Rogers, The Plainsman, Wild Bill Hickok, Restless Gun,* and a small *Dagger/Derringer,* circa 1950s to 1960s.

Group of die cast cap guns showing good likeness to the Colt Peacemaker, Colt Navy and Remington double derringer. Collection: Bruce Thalberg.

Chapter Twentythree

Miscellaneous

Some things just don't fit neatly into one particular category or another. Wonderful cowboy and Western related items which fill out the edges of the canvas and may fit loosely within a definition of folk art, but not always. This chapter is devoted to whatever is left but cannot be left out.

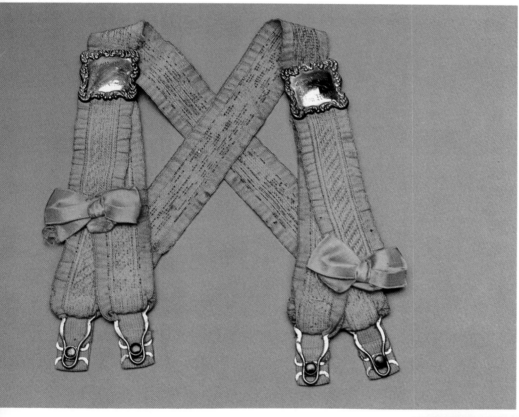

Victorian garter belt, with silver engraved clasps probably was worn by a "fancy" lady of the evening. Silver engraved clasps. Collection: Vic Williams.

> *Some of those girls in Miles City were famous, like Cowboy Annie and Connie the Cowboy Queen. Connie had a $250 dress embroidered with all the different brands-they said there wasn't an outfit from the Yellowstone down to the Platte, and over in the Dakotas too, that couldn't find it's brand on that dress.*
>
> *We Pointed Them North*

Wells Fargo trade sign. Turn of the century. Collection: Dennis Kurlander.

Silver and gold concho of extraordinary quality, depicting a coyote howlng at the moon. Circa 1930-1940. Collection: High Noon.

Nineteenth century wall pocket in original old red paint. What makes this unique is that when closely examined, one can make out the stylized image of a Buffalo's head. Collection: Michael Friedman.

Old pewter flask with engraved image of an "old timer." The squashed appearance indicates this piece resided in a back pocket for a long time. Circa 1900-1910. Collection: Michael Friedman.

Hand-tooled leather picture frame marked "Gallup & Frazier, Pueblo Colorado." Collection: C.W. Lyle, Jr.

Late nineteenth century photo album depicting an express rider. Victorian albums of this type are rare when found with their original base. Collection: Mr. & Mrs. John Schorsch.

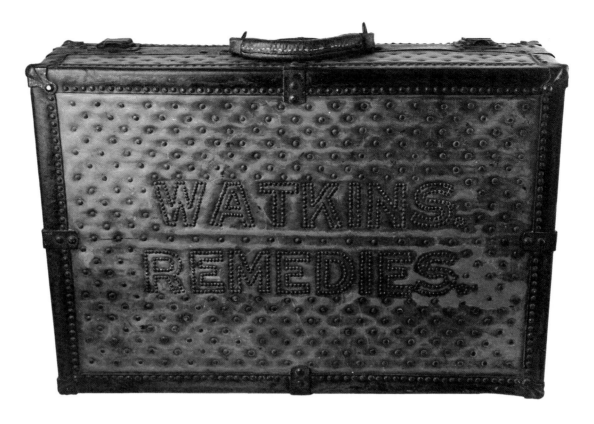

A Watkins Remedies salesman's sample suitcase heavily studded with brass tacks. J.R. Watkins & Co. of Winona, Minn. was a distributor of spices and extracts. Collection: High Noon.

A fob with a pearl buckle and an ivory carving of a horse. Fob with cast brass bronco buster. Collection: C.W. Lyle, Jr.

A watch fob made of sterling silver, circa 1913. Chief Iron Tail of the 101 Ranch Wild West is on the front of the Indian head nickel and the 101 Ranch Bison is on the back. Collection: Ruth and Jerry Murphey.

A watch fob, circa early 1900s, advertising Tenison Bros. saddlery of Dallas, Texas. Collection: Vic Williams.

Well-done, life-sized folk art steer head, carved and painted wood with real horns, made around the turn of the century. Photo: G. Kangas. Collection: Gene and Linda Kangas.

This small enamelled panel mounted on a velvet frame appears to be just a pretty lady, but cover the head and you see a pornographic image. This type of risqué art also appeared on trade mirrors. Collection: Roger Baker.

Brass and steel horseshoe mirror, circa 1900. Collection: Michael Friedman.

Twentieth Century

Known as "pulp art" these paintings were done for covers of dime novels and magazines. Circa 1940-1950. Collection: Michael Friedman.

A barbed wire stretcher, patented January 15, 1895. Collection: Vic Williams.

Chinese silk rug of a steer-wrestler made for the American market, good quality, circa 1940s. Collection: Steve Hofheimer.

Hopalong Cassidy clock, circa 1940s, hard to find in this condition. Collection: Michael Friedman.

The second hand on this Roy Rogers clock is actually an animated Roy Rogers on Trigger, circa 1950s. Collection: Michael Friedman.

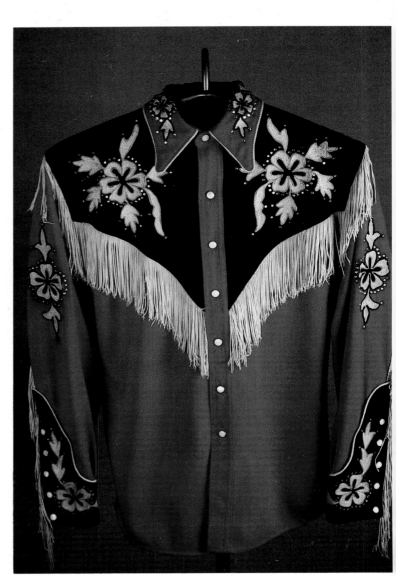

(detail of back of shirt) Wool gabardine Rodeo Queen outfit, shirt and pants. Multicolored embroidery of flowers is on the front of the shirt, and a large butterfly is on the back. Flowers down the sides of the pants have rhinestones. This outfit was worn by a Rodeo Queen in Utah, circa late-1940s or '50's and was made by Vaquero Fashions, Taylor-Berke in California. Collection: High Noon.

Wool gabardine fancy embroidered cowboy shirt and pants. Representative of the best of type, outfits of this quality and condition are hard to find, circa 1940s to 1950s, made by Faye Ward, N.Y. Collection: Michael Friedman.

(front of shirt)

Opposite page:
Advertisement for Merita bread, in good condition and scarce. The lithographed tin sign is actually embossed from behind to give The Lone Ranger and the loaf of bread a three demensional appearance, circa 1950s. Collection: Michael Friedman.

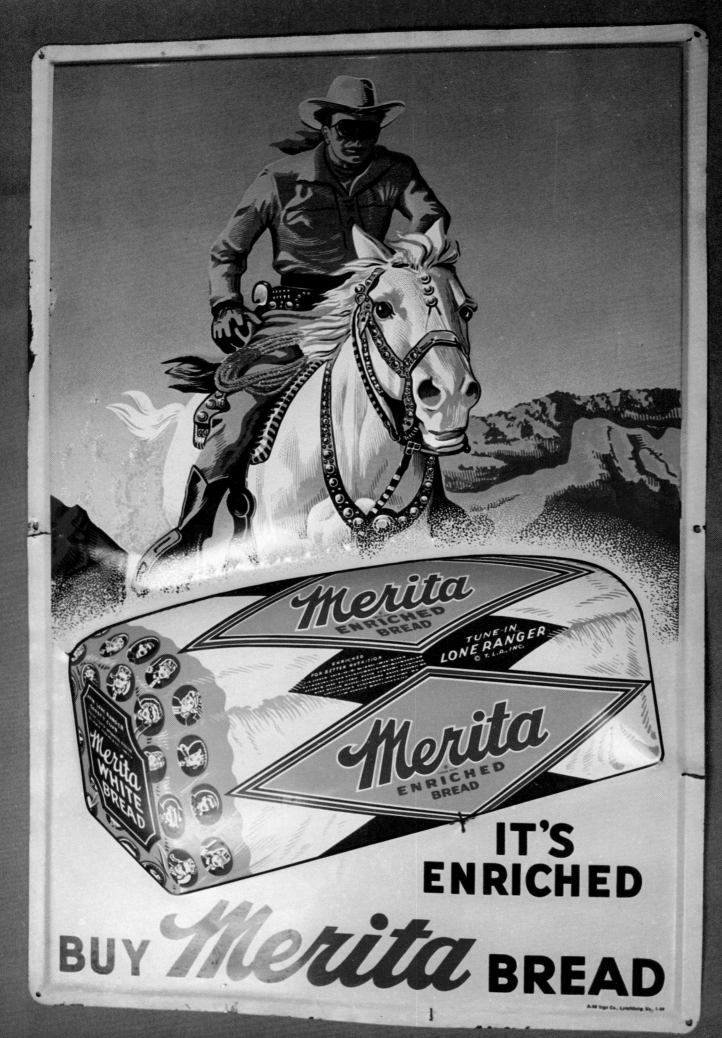

Whimsical cowboy lamp, typically found in a young boy's bedroom in the 1950s. Collection: Steve Hofheimer.

Late 19th century ladies change purse depicting a cowgirl with her horse. Collection: Michael Friedman.

Water sprinkler in the form of a cowboy, circa 1950s. Collection: Alex Shear.

Two of the more desirable Hollywood cowboy lunchboxes, circa 1950s. Collection: Michael Friedman.

Bronco buster by Paul Herzel. This nicely detailed casting was either made as a sculpture or a bookend. Circa 1940s. Collection: Michael Friedman.

Life size, painted, wooden cut-out of a cowboy, probably from an amusement park, circa 1930 to 1940. Collection: Steve Hofheimer.

Cast iron cowboy bottle opener from San Antonio. Collection: Michael Friedman.

Believe it or not, these two posteriors are actually bottle openers. Collection: Michael Friedman.

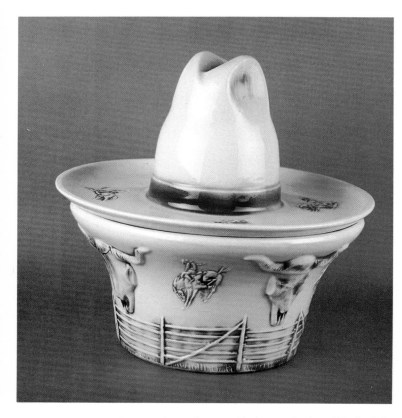

The hat is the lid to this cowboy cookie jar, and when lifted off it doubles as a serving tray, circa 1940s. Collection: Michael Friedman.

Hotel lobby butler depicting a vaquero. Circa 1930. Collection: Michael Friedman.

Cookie Wagon made by Mc Coy Manufacturing Co., circa 1940s. Collection: Michael Friedman.

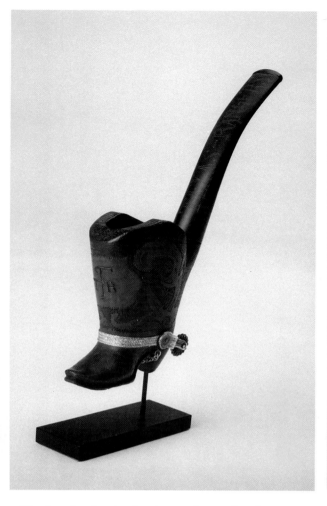

Handmade pipe in the shape of a cowboy boot with silver spur. Stem is inscribed "Texas Ranger" as is the front of the pipe along with its owner's initials. Collection: Michael Friedman.

One of a pair of cowboy bookends in mint condition, circa 1950s. In the heyday of the Hollywood cowboy, manufacturers used the cowboy motif in hundreds of different items. Bookends were a popular form for both Cowboys and Indians. Collection: George and Pattie Schwartz.

The star of Texas and the Texas longhorn distinguish this iron doorstop, circa 1930s to 1940s. Collection: Michael Friedman.

Interesting turn-of-the-century steer horn hat rack. Collection: Michael Friedman.

Polychrome wooden folk carving
found in Fargo, North Dakota, circa
1890-1900. Collection: Dave Wooley.
Photo: Anne Lennox.

Polychrome wooden folk carving
from Thief River Fall, Minnesota,
circa 1930's. Collection: Dave
Wooley. Photo: Anne Lennox.

Bibliography

CATALOGS

Visalia Stock Saddle Co. Catalogue, No.22. 1923 Catalogue. Reprint. San Gabriel, California: Pitman's Treasures & Co., 1989.

August Buermann Mfg. Co., Illustrated Catalogue No. 35. Newark, New Jersey.

"Coggshall Saddles, No. 26." Miles City Saddlery Co. 1925 Catalog. Reprint. San Gabriel, California: Pitman's Treasures & Co., 1989.

"Cowboy Brand." Main-Winchester-Stone Co. 1905 Catalog, No. 35. San Gabriel, California: Pitman's Treasures & Co., 1989.

"D.E. Walker's Genuine Visalia Saddles." 1900 Illustrated Catalogue. Visalia Stock Saddle Co. Reprint. New York: Zon International Publishing Co., 1991.

"Fine Saddles, Bits & Spurs." Butterfield & Butterfield Auction Catalog, November 21, 1989. Rolandesign, 1991.

"Hand Forged Bits One-Piece Spurs. M. Morales Illustrated Catalog No. 5, 1925. Reprint. San Gabriel, California: Pitman's Treasures & Co., 1987.

"Meana Saddles." F.A. Meana 1923 Catalog and C.S. Garcia's Illustrated Catalogue, 1908. San Gabriel, California: Pitman's Treasures & Co., 1990.

"Scrutinizing Bits and Spurs of an Innovative Creator." A J.R. McChesney Manual.

Persimmon Hill. Volume 19, Number 1, Spring 1991. Oklahoma: National Cowboy Hall of Fame and Western Heritage Center, 1991.

Phillips & Gutierrez Catalog and Price List. Reprint. Burbank, California: Reproductions West, 1982.

1927 Catalog. Edward H. Bohlin, Master Craftsman for the Cowboy Kings. Reprint. San Gabriel, California: Pitman's Treasures & Co., 1988.

BOOKS

Abbott, E.C., and Helena Huntington Smith, *We Pointed Them North*, University of Oklahoma Press, 1939.

Adams, Ramon F. *The Old-Time Cowhand.* New York: The MacMillan Company, 1961.

Ahlborn, Richard E., ed. *Man Made Mobile Early Saddles of Western North America.* Washington, D.C.: Smithsonian Institution Press, 1980.

Andrist, Ralph K. and the editors of *American Heritage. The California Gold Rush.* New York: American Heritage Publishing Co., Inc., 1961.

Brown, Mark H. and W.R. Felton. *Before Barbed Wire.* New York: Bramhall House, 1956. ·

Cunningham. Eugene. *Triggernometry, A Gallery of Gunfighters.* Idaho: The Caxton Printers, Ltd., 1941.

Dary, David. *Cowboy Culture.* Kansas: University Press of Kansas, 1981, 1989.

Davis, Marc. "Reopening the Sixteen to One Gold Mine." *Rock & Gem* (July, 1991).

Evans, Paul. "Gold Quartz: The Jewelry of San Francisco." *Spinning Wheel Antiques & Early Crafts*, Vol. 33 (May, 1977); 8-10.

Flayderman, Norman. *Flayderman's Guide to American Firearms...and Their Values*, DB1 Books Inc., 1977, Northbrook, IL.

Forbis, William H. and the editors of Time-Life Books. *The Cowboy.* New York: Time-Life Books, 1973.

Freedman, Russell. *Cowboys of the Wild West.* New York: Clarion Books, 1985.

Hardy, William P. *A Chronology of the Old West.* New York: Vantage Press, Inc., 1988.

Kirkland, K.D., *America's Premier Gunmakers, Winchester*, Exeter Books, New York, 1989.

Kopec, Graham, and Moore, *A Study of the Colt Single Action Army Revolver*, John A. Kopec Publications, Whitmore, CA, 1976.

Various. *Old West Antiques and Collectibles.* Austin, Texas: Great American Publishing Co., 1979.

Mackin, Bill. *Cowboy and Gunfighter Collectibles.* Missoula: Mountain Press Publishing Company, 1989.

Nevin, David and the editors of Time-Life Books. *The Texans.* New York: Time-Life Books, 1975.

Patterson, Richard. *Wyoming's Outlaw Days.* Boulder, Colorado: Johnson Books, 1982.

Pattie, Jane, *Cowboy Spurs and Their Makers.* Texas: Texas A & M University Press, 1991.

Rice, Lee M. and Glenn R. Vernam. *They Saddled the West.* Cambridge, Maryland: Cornell Maritime Press, Inc., 1975.

Rosa, Joseph G. *Guns of the American West.* New York: Exeter Books, 1988.

Russell, Don. *The Wild West.* Fort Worth, Texas: Amon Carter Museum of Western Art, 1970.

Slatta, Richard W. *Cowboys of the Americas.* New Haven and London: Yale University Press, 1990.

Taylor, Lonn and Ingrid Maar. *The American Cowboy.* Washington, D.C.: American Folklife Center, 1983.

Time-Life Books, ed. *The Gamblers.* Alexandria, Virginia: Time-Life Books, 1978.

Trachtman, Paul and the editors of Time-Life Books. *The Gunfighters.* Alexandria, Virginia: Time-Life Books, 1974.

Ward, Don and the editors of *American Heritage. Cowboys and the Cattle Country.* New York: American Heritage Publishing Co., Inc., 1961.

VIDEO

Son of a Gun or How Samuel Colt Changed America, BBC and Song Corp of America, 1987.

Index

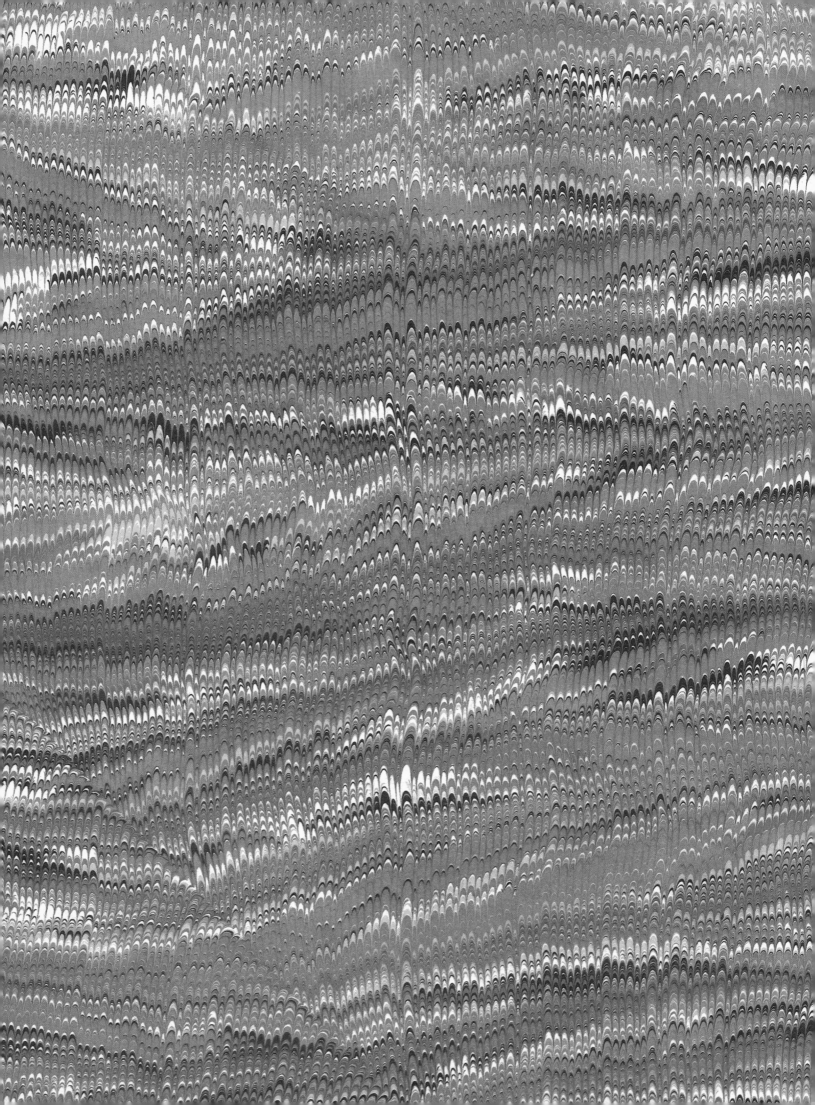